SON OF A POSTMAN

DELIVERING STRAIGHT TALK ON MANAGING FLUFFERS, BULLIES AND THE REST OF THE TEAM

KEVIN R ALGER

*For all the people who have survived my tutelage
and moved on to their own success.*

Perhaps one day I'll work for one of them.

FOREWORD

That Kevin shares his last name with Horatio Alger, famed author of the mythical caricature of American success, may be nothing more than a funny coincidence. It does not seem a coincidence though, because like his "cousin" Horatio, Kevin's story of success is grounded in hard work, industriousness and a strong determination to succeed. But I learned in working for Kevin that this is not a story he cares to tell at length. He would much rather tell you about something amazing one of "his people" just did, because Kevin has a passion for the people he works with and one of his greatest prides is in putting together a team where individuals and team succeed together. Kevin is the practiced manager *par excellence*.

In *Son of A Postman*, Kevin shares some of his best thinking about how to become a successful leader and manager. In the book, as in conversation, Kevin moves quickly from topic to topic and story to story, forming a patchwork of reflections on thirty two years of managing hundreds of people in places all around the United States and the world. With good humor and candor Kevin describes his experiences facing common management challenges and the practical lessons he learned along the way to becoming a great manager.

By recounting his own personal experiences, Kevin creates a practical guide that is as useful as it is humorous, heartfelt and full of Kevin's big personality. The influence of Grandma Ruth in his life, as readers will learn, made him quite the wit, no stranger to plain and occasionally frank language and inclined to thoughtfully "tell it like it is." That influence is as apparent in this book as it was in the leadership style I witnessed while working for him.

Perhaps best of all, Kevin's anecdotal style makes the book accessible to the everyday practitioner as well as to management gurus and academics. I myself, as a person who continues to aspire to become a better leader and as a former employee and student of Kevin, frequently find myself recalling in my day to day work the very same lessons he captures in the book.

So, whether facing a tough management challenge or simply looking for tips from a veteran on how to polish your leadership style, *Son of A Postman* is a great reference. And no matter what you manage – whether it is a sports team, a classroom full of screaming students or a meeting room full of screaming adults –Kevin's recipe for successful management has something for everyone. And that is why *Son of A Postman* manages to deliver.

> *A lifetime apprentice,*
> *who chooses to remain anonymous*

AUTHOR'S NOTE

People kept calling me, wanting to talk.

"Can we meet for lunch? I have something to ask you."

"Are you free for 15 minutes? I want to check in with you."

"I'm dying to hear what you have to say about this crazy career opportunity."

It's happened over and over again and it still happens. It comes from all over the world. People come to me for guidance. People come to me for help with networking. Usually it's about their career. Sometimes it's about other parts of their lives. It's been like this for years.

"Let's have dinner. I need some honest advice."

I realize and am honored by the trust that underlies these requests. It's something that grew naturally over my years of leading people, always with an eye out for their success. In my world, what matters is helping people to learn well, to develop their abilities, to excel in their work and then to be rewarded for it. More than the process or the product, throughout my working life I have always put the emphasis on the person.

I cared about their next promotion, the higher salary or the bonus, but that was only part of it. Much more, I used my experience and expertise to coach people on their way to greater achievements and to teach them how to do the same for others.

As I developed a reputation for being a good leader, I became the go-to guy for advice – for the junior person new to her career, for the mid-level manager stumbling in his development and even for the experienced executive seeking how to help her company or her group. In time, it became a wide-ranging and loyal following.

The more this kept happening, the more I thought it would be a good idea to put together a book of my ideas about managing people. I pulled together my own thoughts and supplemented them with the experiences of many people I interviewed from various industries and professions. With the exception of my own family members, the genders, details and locations in the stories I tell throughout the book have sometimes been altered.

This is not a textbook. It takes a very practical approach, drawing on my experiences and using anecdotes to teach, just as I do in real life. It's for all the people who think, "No one ever taught me how to lead people."

This could be a new leader who is smart, competent, and ambitious and hardworking. She has performed well in her job and been asked to manage others. Now she feels unprepared. Her challenges are no longer the familiar ones of using her own skills and knowledge to produce results, devise a clever strategy or win a client. Her personal accomplishments are no longer the whole story.

Or it could be a guy who has to take on responsibility for the work of others. He needs to learn how to put together an effective group and help them produce. He must figure out how to motivate and evaluate the members of his team.

This is to serve as a guide in doing all those things. It's for anyone who realizes she has a deficit as a leader and wants to improve. It's for everyone who delights in seeing others succeed. The more I reflected on what I had to say, I realized that, as much as it applies to managers in business, it also applies to any leader of people in any context. It's for everyone who wants – or needs – to lead as a parent, teacher, coach, or executive and for those who are already leaders but want to improve.

Most of all, it is to help anyone find out how to be happy in the success of others and to help them to discover, as I have, the joys and satisfactions in doing that well.

Since I decided to write this book I have travelled a great deal around world, for business, for yoga retreats, to visit an ashram in India and to see friends. I found that when I described what I was writing about, no matter the person I was talking with, the response was overwhelmingly, "Great! I can really use that!"

I heard this from a shoe designer, a Hong Kong banker, a doctor who runs a multi-practice office, a textile manufacturer, the leader of an animal protection agency, the manager of a yoga studio, more than one CEO, a school principal and lots of other professionals.

During the course of writing, I have continued to get email and phone calls from people seeking advice. They say, "Hey, Kevin, I really need that book."

I'm happy that it's now ready and I hope it delivers what they want.

I feel fortunate to have been a mentor to so many talented people. It has been tremendously satisfying to watch them achieve successes of their own. It's also great fun.

KEVIN'S WORLD

CHAPTER 1

NO MOTHER TERESA

NEW YORK CITY, NEW YORK. I'm sitting in a very crowded conference room on a high floor of an office building located in the middle of Manhattan. This room, these people, these speakers, this gathering – in some form this scene is played out in organizations all across the world. "Management" touts the benefits of such assemblies: the camaraderie, the efficiencies, the positive impact on whatever it is that is defined as "success."

Personally, I use these frequent and seemingly endless meetings to people watch. I habitually scan the room to check out new looks, weight gain, hair loss, facelifts and all kinds of other details. I also use them to stay connected to the many colleagues who, at one time or another, I have managed, mentored, fired, promoted or savored their success.

My idea of success is very clear. Of course, there are those who measure it by money and power. I liked that when it came my way just as much as anyone. The profits and bonuses and promotions all serve to underscore good performance.

Yet it didn't take long to figure out that a much greater sense of fulfillment comes from the accomplishments that contribute to the wellbeing of the business. A particular pride comes from producing outstanding products that both do well and at the same time illuminate our brilliance. I found this all quite satisfying for a good while and it motivated me to many worthy triumphs.

Over time, though, I found there is another level in the hierarchy of success that rings more true for me. From where I stand now, having reached the high rungs of a universally respected global financial institution, I recognize that the greatest satisfaction comes with being able to help others achieve their own advancement. The enduring idea of "success" for me has come from teaching people, investing in them for the long term, offering them guidance as they make their way on their path and making them happy. I do believe this is pretty unusual in most industries, but especially so in the financial world, where the bullies can be cutthroat and all too ready to use others solely for their own elevation.

Don't be misled. I am no Mother Teresa. For 32 years, I have worked in the financial services industry and for a single firm, at which I have reached the senior ranks. I have thrived in this industry with somewhat sharp elbows and I am just as keen to win as all those around me. Some refer to me as "The Fixer" or "The Ax Man" and some accuse me of having a "fast hook" with limited tolerance for slackers.

Monikers aside, I have managed many businesses and made tough decisions while developing a strong and long-lasting following of former employees and colleagues. I have given guidance to many promising individuals in the offices I have managed all over the world. I have then watched them leave my tutelage to thrive – at my firm, with competitors and in other industries. I don't think there is one person I could not call today to catch up, laugh, network, refer people or consult. There are countless people around the world who are alumni of "Kevin's World." These people are the reason I have so much enjoyed my working life.

Somehow along the way I developed a strong reputation as being a "good" manager. I like to think of my talent as more akin to being a decisive, honest teacher. As my reputation grew, I became a magnet for talented young people who knew I would guide and teach them and then actively encourage them to move to their next opportunity. I love saying to a person new to my world, "The sooner I get rid of you, the happier I will be." Truth is, I mean it. I believe it to be an important measure of my success as a manager and a crucial ingredient for the long-term retention of valuable colleagues. I look every day for chances to identify and train my replacement and I make that known often.

Just like teaching children, leading people to success follows from explicitly encouraging them to expand outside of their comfort zones. This approach has merit far beyond the financial world, beyond corporations and business organizations into all parts of life where mentors and leaders guide those who are developing. It applies to parents, teachers, coaches, team captains, managers, executives and leaders of all kinds all over the world.

Although I have worked for one firm for my entire career, I have had many distinct roles and they have molded the "character" I am today. I have managed junior and senior people, product makers, mathematicians, traders, sales people, Americans, Europeans, Latins, Asians, and I even managed a business of a thousand people primarily populated with lawyers. Good thing I had lost my hair and was over 50 at the time or I would have had no respect from that crew!

Now, after an almost fairy-tale career in business, I have decided to pack it in. As I embark on a new journey, my first step is to document in this book my insights and ideas about mentoring and managing people. I will tell about the path I took as a Postman's son, about Grandma Ruth and the other important influences along the way and about the many lessons I learned.

Back to my meeting here in the conference room: I just spoke. The crowd's reaction says they found it compelling and inspiring. I now return to a contemplation of the hair color chosen by the woman sitting to my left.

CHAPTER 2

SON OF A POSTMAN

GENEVA, SWITZERLAND. I have arrived at the top of an escalator inside a shopping mall on the outskirts of the city. I am here to visit one of the offices of the global financial services company that employs me. Whenever I come to Switzerland, I am reminded of the Swiss reputation for planning and efficiency. I often admire how they do their careful planning, protect that good reputation and keep everything so clean.

I can see my reflection in the mirrored revolving doors that are the entrance to the office. These are one-way mirrors, allowing the receptionist inside to see who is approaching. This is one of the larger offices globally and the only one I have been to that is in a shopping mall. It is also the only one that seems to take such a thoughtful precaution to preserve privacy by making sure the mall shoppers can't gaze into the offices to watch the employees or clients.

Inside, the receptionist gives me a warm greeting. I have observed that she has the ability to remember the names of pretty much everyone who visits there. She comes from behind the desk to give me a big hug and three cheek kisses. (She does this the Swiss way, not to be confused with the two kisses in London or the three in Paris that start on a different cheek.)

At the small elevator bank inside the office, I notice the activities display and I see my name in bold letters on the visitor list welcoming me to Geneva. Such efficiency! Wouldn't it be nice if we were all so well organized and had such clear plans for our lives?

LOTS OF LUCK

I think that my family home was run pretty efficiently when I was growing up. Our daily family schedule was carried out with precision and with little room for delays. I realized much later in life the influence of all that planning and discipline on my educational and career successes.

Most success stories are part luck and part common sense, supported by a strong work ethic and either knowledge or a willingness to learn. The luck part may include your genetic make-up and being born into a family where you can learn by example. I know I had the luck part. I have found that the knowledge part is the easiest to gain and is possessed by many. Success can also be facilitated by personal connections, family history and a prestigious education. I had none of those advantages.

In my case, there was no planning for a career in the financial or any other industry. It all just happened in the ebb and flow of life. Even as late as when I graduated from college, my knowledge of the financial world extended only to the local bank branch where I maintained a small checking account. There were no early yearnings to chase a financial job and its pot of gold.

I grew up in working-class Philadelphia in the 1960s and '70s. The second oldest of four children, two girls and two boys, I was the first in my very large extended family to go to college. Frankly, there was not much thought about where I would go. There were no visits to target schools and no consideration of my living on any campus. On my own, I applied to a few local schools and got into one or two. I chose LaSalle College in North Philadelphia. It was a very simple decision, given that I could commute from my parents' house and that it was a Catholic college. Up until then, all of my education had been in Catholic schools. I believe their strong emphasis on memorization helped me develop an ability to remember things that still seems to amaze other people.

As soon as I was admitted to LaSalle, my parents started to wonder and worry about how we were going to afford the 1977 tuition of $3,000 per year. For my entire four years of college, I had a full-time night job in order to pay that tuition. I worked the 4:00 p.m. to 12:00 midnight shift at a community hospital. My role there was to restock and deliver medical supplies used throughout the hospital. I did this with Swiss efficiency. As soon as I arrived at work, I would get all my daily stock work completed at rapid speed. Then I was free to spend the later part of the night doing my college studying, as my only other responsibilities were to be available as needed to deliver randomly requested special supplies, assemble orthopedic equipment when a new patient was admitted and transport the bodies of patients who either arrived dead or passed away on my shift. It was all pretty interesting and I did consider becoming a hospital administrator.

BANK TELLER

There was very little discussion at home about what you would do for work. Rather, all discussions centered on a goal to do a little better than your parents and perhaps buy a "single house." Of course, there was a desire to get a job with a "big concern" that also provided "hospitalization." In 1981, the aim was to have the security of working at a large firm and that was really all my family knew.

Once, someone in our neighborhood won $25,000 in the lottery and we all thought he was set for life. I can very clearly remember thinking, back then, that I would be so happy to one day earn $50,000. I really never did think about salary when I was considering my college major or my future. I now think that it was a healthy way to do things. Today, there is so much specific planning and pressure to decide about a career without really experiencing a broad array of options. I picked Finance and Management as a major mostly because I realized I really did not want to study Accounting or Pre-Med, which were the other two choices I considered. I had no career plan.

My father was the only child in his family but my mother had 12 siblings. All of them grew up in Philadelphia in a family that had been there for several generations and all but two of them stayed to raise their families and live their lives in the area. I have more than 100 cousins and second cousins. Like me, most of this Irish Catholic crowd had very little exposure to life outside of this local world and none had anything to do with the financial industry.

For a long time, family members would ask my siblings, "Is Kevin still a bank teller in New York?" We often laugh about how my sisters would say yes or, later, tell them that I had become the Head Teller. My parents always struggled to explain what it is that I actually do all day. Most of the relatives sort of wonder when they hear I am in Kuwait, Sao Paulo or Singapore, could it be that I am at classes to learn how to count foreign currency?

As I was finishing college with a Finance and Management degree in the Class of 1981, I became obsessed with finding a job other than the one I had in the hospital. I desperately wanted to move to New York City from Philadelphia. After 22 years under the heavy hand of a Catholic education and living with my parents, my goal was to start a different life. The hospital did offer me a full time position as a purchasing agent for hospital supplies and equipment but I declined. I wanted a new adventure.

MASS MAILING

I spent months blindly sending resumes to any company that advertised in the *Wall Street Journal* and that also had an address in New York City. Sure, there were local Philadelphia companies recruiting at my small college but there was little chance any of them would land me in New York City. Sadly, it is largely still true that many of the most sought-after companies recruit only at the "best" schools.

I mailed more than a thousand resumes in my self-placement campaign. I did find it odd at the time that my college classmates did not seem to share my sense of urgency but I continued with my mission nonetheless. It was the first time I was conscious that perhaps I had an above-average level of ambition or motivation. The four years of college, combined with my full-time hospital job, had developed my abilities to spin many plates, meet deadlines, make decisions quickly and practice other high-productivity skills. There was no time to do otherwise! It also set me up for a lifetime of requiring little sleep.

My first job in New York City was as a buyer-in-training in the woman's shoe department for Lord & Taylor department store. Frankly, it was the only job offer I received. Reality is that I probably would be there still had it not been that, six weeks into it, I received a telephone call from the human resources department of the firm that was to become my sole employer. They were seeking a junior analyst.

I did not have to give the opportunity a lot of thought. Although I did not really know what the company did, or what being a junior analyst meant, I understood that they were offering me a $14,000 annual salary and that was better than the $12,000 I was earning as a shoe buyer. The additional $2,000 was enough for me to decide. So I took the job.

NO FUTURE

There are three notable things about my getting that initial job. First, my father took the call from the recruiter and to the day he died he reminded me of how he "got me the job!"

Second, I think it is important to mention that this recruiter was the recipient of one of my thousand resumes, proving my direct marketing campaign successful.

Third, the human resources guy who hired me told me repeatedly that I was being hired for " just this job." Several times he stressed that I should not expect any training or promotions, because my background did not qualify me for such advancements. Generally, things are not like that anymore but times were different then. I remember that conversation very clearly. I even remember that I was wearing a blue shirt and a yellow tie. Back in 1981, yellow ties were required interview garb. Someone later told me that I got the job because I dressed well.

Clearly, I didn't heed any of the admonitions of the "inspirational" HR fellow but I have not forgotten him. In fact, I have spent the last 30 years making sure that those who excel are recognized, trained and promoted, regardless of their background.

Perhaps my landing that job illustrates the luck part of success but there have been three other important aspects of my development that have shaped me into an effective manager. I have leveraged a strong work ethic, an almost genetic desire to be a teacher and finally some combination of emotional intelligence and common sense. I have a pretty good sense of how I developed the first two of these. A discussion of the third would require a deep psychological analysis of my childhood that would surely cause you to shut this book!

DO AS I DO

Growing up and during my early adult life, I often thought about how my father was rarely around. I used to think I was deprived and that he didn't contribute much to my development. Then at some point as an adult, I realized his very crucial contribution.

My father was a Postman and for all of the 22 years I lived under his roof, he also worked a second job. Our family had a very disciplined routine that revolved around his work schedule. He went to be the Postman at 5:00 a.m. each day and delivered the mail until he returned at 3:00 p.m. He then napped until 4:00, at which time the entire family was required to be at dinner, prepared by my mother. My father then left the house at 4:40 for his second job working a five-hour shift at the Sears catalog center where he boxed up and shipped off items people had ordered. He returned each night at the end of his shift, arriving home at exactly 10:10 p.m.

This was possibly the best demonstration of work ethic that I ever could have had. His example is why I was able to excel in college while simultaneously working a full-time job and then do the same later in business school. I count these lessons, delivered by example straight from the Postman to me, among the most valuable of my life. My father wasn't there physically preaching to me but rather showing me every day through his actions how work gets done. I never would have survived in the corporate world without his example, especially given some of the headwinds I faced in my early days.

That work ethic and my experience in my hospital job during college became very useful later, when I went to business school in the evenings during the first few years of my career as a "bank teller." I wasn't actually a bank teller ever but my early roles did not have demanding hours. As a consequence, I was able to shine as the number cruncher for a few senior people and then, a few nights a week, head out of the office to attend class at Fordham University Graduate School of Business Administration. (More Catholic education!) My firm was very supportive of employees going to business school and paid the tuition.

THE TEACHING GENE

Once the daily dinner was completed at 4:30, my mother would require her four children to assemble at the dining room table for our homework session. These sessions took place as far back as I can remember. I participated from the time I was in first grade and each sibling joined this routine as soon as he or she entered school. My mother was innately a teacher and she was a strict disciplinarian about our homework. She would sit there with us as we did our math and spelling drills and not let one of us leave the table until all of us had completed our assignments. If home schooling had been popular back then, we all could have been educated at home.

Again learning by example, I gained a powerful sense of responsibility, attention to detail and honoring of deadlines, as well as the experience of having a teacher who cares. I am sure this is why both of my sisters are elementary school teachers today and my brother and I have both been managers of many people.

I have observed that the most consistently successful managers are those with a keen awareness of their responsibility to teach their employees. They understand that this is fundamental and needs to be done every day. Unfortunately, many managers don't recognize the benefits of teaching but focus more on just using their employees' hard work to help elevate their own stature. I am sure that they miss out on the best aspect of their job.

BOTTOM TO TOP

The final ingredient to my success is what I believe to be an optimal combination of empathy and common sense. I am no expert on Emotional Intelligence, but I typically score very high on those tests, plus people often tell me I have it and I accept that as true.

What I do consistently, perhaps somewhat uniquely, is to work equally with people at all levels of a hierarchy. I spend focused, personal time with everyone from the bottom level up to the top and I always make sure to have time for anyone who needs it. This way, I can attend to the details of each person's work and provide real-time feedback. It also communicates to them and to the others in their group that each one is a valuable team member. Many times I've been told how much this has meant to my crew and how it makes them feel good.

I am also a huge proponent of grooming people, regardless of their job level, to move to their next role and then helping them make that move.

15

WHATEVER IT TAKES

My own first role as a junior analyst was a position low down near the bottom of the corporate ladder. My attitude right from the start was that I was willing to take on anything I was asked to do. I know it is because of that attitude that I moved along from job to job and gained broad experience along the way. Gradually I took on responsibilities for managing portfolios of stocks and managing client accounts.

Those were the days when stock trading was evolving from depending almost solely on qualitative scrutiny by traders to using the analysis of numbers to identify opportunities for buying and selling. It was becoming less an art and more a science. These changes led to high-volume trading and that required a whole new way of doing things. My managers asked me to figure out how to run this business and, with that request, another new job evolved for me. Of course I approached it with the view that I would "do whatever it takes" to meet this challenge and I invented some striking seat-of-the-envelope, back-of-the-pants approaches. I became the head of trading not by seeking it out but because that was where my winding path led.

Over the decades, I progressed through many more roles, reached the level of Managing Director and became the CEO of various global businesses. All of this involved the management of thousands of people worldwide. (Back home, my siblings tracked my advancement for the rest of the family, reporting my promotions from bank teller through the ranks until I finally reached a big job as Branch Manager!)

None of my successes came as a result of deliberate planning. Instead, my accomplishments at every level were the result of taking action, always with an unconstrained willingness to do "whatever it takes." This meant that whenever I was asked to move to a different role, I said yes. I wasn't afraid.

My responsibilities have taken me to virtually every part of the world, from the Middle East to Asia, Europe and Latin America. I have worked with all types of people, from trust fund babies to billionaire entrepreneurs to sovereign government officials. I have met with corporate executives and religious leaders throughout the U.S., as well as with horribly inter-bred eccentrics. I even have a colleague who is a real life cowgirl! I have enjoyed a life I never could have imagined.

FIDGET

How did I get to become a "manager" and "leader?" In my family, there were definitely no planning meetings that required sitting in a room for endless hours. You may think that I have become used to this from my many years working in a corporate business environment. Well, you would be wrong. I have spent much of my career trying to avoid such sessions because I find it difficult to pay sustained attention. I have always wondered about the effectiveness of all-day meetings, the length of the average person's attention span and the most common nap times.

In fact, for most of my adult life I have annoyed people with my fidgeting. All during my childhood, I drove my parents crazy because I was pretty much incapable of sitting still for more than 10 minutes. Starting at age nine I took drum lessons and later evolved into a pretty accomplished percussionist. This was my parents' very creative solution to dealing with my ADHD or whatever they thought my disorder might be in those days. You know that if I were a nine-year-old today I would be stuffed full of pills.

EARLY SIGNS

There are many stories of the early signs of my management flair, but there are three in particular that I like best.

The first is that as a child I was regularly "playing business." Even back when I was as young as five years old I would assemble all kinds of things that I used as "products." My products could be all the books in the house, the cleaning supplies, my Halloween candy (and sometimes that of my sisters too) or just my toys. I was constantly taking a detailed inventory and making up prices for them. I even once sold some of my sister's toys to a kid in the neighborhood.

The best part of playing business (to me) was that I would require my younger sister to be my secretary. I would set her up in the hall outside of my bedroom. Her desk was a plastic TV table and I made her sit there for hours. I would give her assignments, scold her and then return to my room and slam the door. Happily, I got that management technique out of my system at an early age!

My mother likes to cite the next story, which is about how I used to manage all the kids in the neighborhood. A busy 10-year-old, I was always getting people together and coming up with schemes to have even more gatherings. The thing I did the most was to organize "carnivals," which were like street fairs with contest booths and sideshows. I would take all sorts of things from my house to use as prizes, which typically were things belonging to my three siblings. I remember being especially happy one time when a new family moved into the neighborhood and they had ten children. These kids were fresh faces to become my "employees" and boy were they good. They fell right into line, though I did have to soften my management style. I couldn't hold them captive in my house because there were just too many of them. So I took over their basement and turned that into my headquarters!

The third story happened when I was an adult. It concerns my grandmother, who pointed out a certain trait of mine after years of watching me operate. This was my paternal grandmother, Ruth, who was born and grew up on a farm in rural Virginia in the early 1900s. In 1932, she moved to Philadelphia with my grandfather and their young newborn son, my father. For the rest of her life, she always made reference to that move to the "North." Grandma Ruth kept her southern, farm-girl accent her whole life. She used a multitude of farm expressions and many one-liners that made us all laugh. No surprise that my siblings and I still use these expressions. My sisters actually compiled them and we refer to it as "The Book of Ruth."

Grandma was always "huntin' things up" or complaining that something was "awful sore" and she was unable to pronounce the word "aluminum,." She always had a school-girl giggle. On Christmas mornings, she would look over at me and say, "Kaaavin, it'll all be over soon!" My grandmother and I shared a dislike of crowds and family rituals.

This story is from the time my sister bought a house in downtown Philadelphia, very close to where Grandma Ruth lived. I had organized a few friends to come over to help paint the house. (My sister was a working, single parent then and had no time for any big project like that.) My friends, one visiting from London, were all there with me on a Saturday night when Grandma Ruth came by. She was wearing a very old, tattered, god-awful winter coat and her head was wrapped so tightly in a faux-chiffon scarf that it was "a wonder" she could even hear.

She looked quickly around the room and said, "Kaaavin, there ain't no paint on your brush! You just givin' orders."

I have never been able to decide if this was a further sign of my natural-born management prowess but I have definitely never forgotten Grandma Ruth's admonition and since that day 25 years ago I have always made it a point to have paint on my brush.

THE POSTMAN MOVES ON

I have had a very strong affiliation with one special group all of my life. It is the strongest affiliation I have ever known. My involvement with them molded many of my behaviors and deeply influenced my strongest beliefs. My work ethic, my consideration for others, my interest in helping people to develop and my attention to detail were all learned through my association with these people.

When you have a well-run team, you get more accomplished and it is achieved in a way that can feel pretty easy. If you undertake something extra challenging, you typically get a warm and fuzzy feeling as you reach your goals. When the well-run team is under excess stress, it sometimes does its best work.

My team recently performed exceptionally well under very challenging circumstances. I was highly impressed with the allocation of responsibilities, the equitable distribution of time commitments and the collaborative and informed decision-making. The junior players were also involved. They were fully informed of the goals of the mission and the senior players were mindful of and interested in the junior members' input. I was especially pleased about how we resolved conflicts. The latter is a good measure of the effectiveness of any team.

Perhaps you have figured out that I am speaking of my family and that the recent challenge was the decline and death of my father. We came together and functioned as a well-oiled machine. I realized anew, as we worked our way through those experiences, what a strong foundation my family has given me. I am one very fortunate a Son of A Postman.

CHAPTER 3

THE FIXER

LONDON, ENGLAND. New Yorkers may disagree but London truly is the center of the world, no? I lived in London for two years in the late 1990's. My firm had based me there to be the global head of stock trading, with employees reporting to me from Tokyo, Melbourne, London and New York. Our offices were in the West End, near Buckingham Palace and the theater district. For an expat living in London, there could not have been a better office location.

This was one of the first of the many times that I have been charged with changing the status quo. In these offices, stock trading had been done the in the same way for at least the previous 25 years. I was to find ways to modernize our trading practice. This required that I make major modifications, disrupting a long-established, comfortable routine and changing the way people did their jobs or, in some cases, moving them on to other things.

I know the city well and come here often. I am visiting here now on a business trip combined with an interview to become a board member for an animal rights organization and to visit old friends. It feels like the right place for me to begin to synthesize my ideas about managing people. I have many friends and former colleagues in London, from all walks of life and work, so this is also a good place for me to gather opinions and experiences from others. Before I turn to them, however, it's time for an honest self-assessment.

THE REPUTATION

Over the years, I have been through many job changes, mergers, acquisitions, integrations, consolidations and takedowns. In their various ways, these many assignments all called for attentive and creative management to ensure good outcomes.

My transfer to London those many years ago was a result of my willingness to step into any new role when asked. My attitude was: if there's something new to figure out, I'm interested. The more I was successful, the more my company kept asking me to take on problematic or especially challenging parts of the business and the more I kept on saying yes. It's because of this that I became known as "The Fixer." It's as "The Fixer" that I have developed a clear view of what works in management, not to mention collecting a lot of pretty striking stories.

As you can imagine, one part of being "The Fixer" is to identify and clear out people and processes that are not working well. It was from taking on that role that I also took on the title "Ax Man." Cleaning house can be tough on everyone involved. I learned that the best way to carry out those responsibilities is with straightforward honesty.

As you tear down a broken organization, it is equally important that you have a plan for building a strong new team and a clear idea of what you want it to do. This means evaluating the resources and people you have, recruiting and developing those you'll need, and then moving ahead to implement your plan with close attention to each step along the way.

My many years of doing all this have led to some of my most effective management techniques. My purpose here is to distill those experiences into advice and guidance for the benefit of any manager of people. I have observed that most people "manage" in some way, whether they use that title or not. All teachers and parents are managers because of their functions in life. A parent has to manage her children and keep a household running smoothly. A teacher manages his students and their curriculum, and keeps order in the classroom. In other organizations, a manager's job is to teach and motivate people to be productive and effective in their jobs.

In any business, there are people who are natural managers who evolve into leadership roles and there are those who aspire to be managers who need to be developed and guided. The age-old error that organizations make around the world is moving the best producer into a management role without giving her any training for development. Being a manager or leader requires specific skills and for most people it's not something you just "pick up" as you go about your daily business.

SELF-IMAGE

I have developed a good, long track record of success as a manager. To this day I am surprised by this because I have a self-image as someone more in the supporting category. When I reconcile my self-image with the more objective results, I conclude that a truly effective manager or leader is in fact also a strong and dedicated support person. The more supportive the grand pooh-bah is of those in his charge, the more successful the entire organization becomes.

ALWAYS A BRIDESMAID

A few years ago, when I started to evaluate my life and my long career, I realized that I have often been, and may always be, a bridesmaid. It is actually not a bad role. You get recognized just fine and you get to spend lots of time with all the people in attendance. Your role is to stand by to make sure everything goes smoothly and to make everyone at the event happy. When you're successful, you make the bride look really good.

If you are comfortable with this role for the long term, you can have a wonderful life. It's like teaching, parenting or managing people who are super appreciative or super talented. It's also like always being the best salesperson. It can be very rewarding.

As part of my assessment, I realized that I was susceptible to a good sales job by an effective leader. Such a person is able to sell you a bag of goods that really may not turn out to be as described. I had a history of being willing to fix broken businesses or integrate inefficient operations and when I was being asked to take on yet another Pandora's box, I was usually reminded how good I was at re-energizing dysfunctional teams. While this was both true and flattering, I didn't always carefully consider the impact my decision to say yes might have on me. I was skipping what in my Mindfulness practice is called having compassion for yourself. Even when we are thoughtfully caring and compassionate toward others, we still need to remember to give ourselves a break.

Throughout my life, I have knowingly accepted many a mission without adequately ensuring that the rewards would actually turn out as advertised. Such rewards can be emotional, financial or other factors that bring you satisfaction. The absence of such assurances never really bothered me at decision time, because I loved a new challenge and very much enjoyed the people who thrived under my tutelage. Yet things did not always work out as intended for me personally.

BACKUP SINGER

I confess that, rather than be a star, I have always wanted to be a backup singer for some hip and preferably soulful singer. I think those backups are just the coolest people in the world. To be completely honest, I find the black female backup singers to be especially appealing. I hesitated to tell people that I really want to be a black female backup singer because I could just imagine all the interesting (but incorrect) assumptions and judgments.

Similar to a bridesmaid, a back up singer fills a strong and essential support role. She is crucial to a performer just like the bridesmaid is to the bride or a reliable worker-bee is to a truly successful company.

The truth is, I find self-promotion to be tiring and uncomfortable. Yet I do understand that it's a really important part of many roles. Actually, it's like marketing anything else you believe in. If you want other people to be aware of you and responsive to you, then you really do need to tell them about yourself and what you're doing. In some environments, self-promotion is a central and essential part of the culture. I know I could never be a star in the entertainment business where it is a constant requirement.

THE ANTI-CHRIST?

Some years ago, someone referred to me as the "anti-Christ." Apparently he had some issues with the way I operate. This was not a big surprise to me, as I have always known that my *modus operandi* was not aligned with this person's playbook, priorities or frankly, his ethics. People can always agree to disagree but to label me "anti-Christ" seemed a bit strong, since this was completely unrelated to any religious beliefs. It also had nothing to do with brain surgery, the violation of human rights, solving world hunger or climate change.

Nonetheless, I took what might have been just a passing crack as serious feedback and did a self-audit. Despite my long-time awareness of this individual's distaste for me, and knowing that his opinion was in the minority, I took the verbal attack as a good reminder that perhaps I should work on my "image" a bit.

I have never been skilled at image control. I find it tiring and even somewhat dishonest but am I also fully aware of why you need to be careful with your frankness. There can be such a thing as being too direct in your honesty.

I thought deeply about the meaning behind the "anti-Christ" accusation and what it suggested about my style. I concluded that I was coming across, more than I would like, as too rigid, too rule-abiding and possibly too focused on my own definition of what was "fair." I knew that there would be no change to my fundamental beliefs but I did make a few edits to the way in which I communicate with people. I wanted to minimize any chance of appearing predictable or dogmatic.

I made a careful effort to listen more and to discuss issues more fully. I also softened the bluntness of my candid opinions. I found my new approach was pretty effective. I noticed a shift in the reactions to my comments and an enhanced ability to influence others. My lesson learned was that it is important to manage your communication style.

MAKING A DIFFERENCE

I believe that there is a way for everyone to succeed if we thoughtfully guide him or her to the right place. No matter who they are, they depend in part on the role models available to them. Being a good role model is another big reason to be in charge of your image.

Their progress also depends on the feedback they get and the quality of the teachers, coaches, managers and leaders who help them along. So while I hope to entertain you with my stories, I also hope to help you gain some new tools and habits that will improve your ability to organize and motivate those you parent or manage.

For my advice to be helpful and if you hope to be successful, it is imperative that you really want to be a manager. You must believe you can make a difference, both to the people you manage and to the overall success of whatever it is you are aiming to achieve. If your desire to be a manager is just to gain glory or more compensation or to prevent someone else from becoming your boss, it is unlikely that you will succeed. If you have the responsibility to manage people, whether it is your children, your students or your employees, I believe you will have the best outcome when you embrace your role as leader and, more importantly, when you enjoy being a manager.

My goal is to give guidance by relying on real-life stories. (After all, this is meant to be entertaining, not a textbook.) In addition to my own best stories, you'll find some anecdotes about leaders from very different environments and organizations, including a school principal and an army general and others I have interviewed from a variety of industries.

I will lay the foundation of my philosophy of leadership along with the principles and techniques that I believe will help you manage well, including my management recipe and the special ingredients that make it tasty. I will then identify six Types of people, discuss their characteristics and typical behavior and suggest ways to deal with them.

THE RECIPE

CHAPTER 4

SELECT GOOD SEEDS

LONDON, ENGLAND. Isn't it ironic to be writing a recipe while I'm in London, a city that is not well known for its culinary excellence? I think that is just the right sort of place to be creative. The recipe I have cooked up has six parts that contain my philosophy and advice about leadership and managing. First, you must select good seeds and that is what this chapter is about. Then nourish them, irrigate well, work in the fields, weed them out and finally serve them up.

Remember that the real joy of managing comes when you find your own ways of doing things and then savor the satisfactions that come from seeing them work. It will be best when you find out how to mix up the ingredients of your own recipe to suit your personal style.

BUILDING YOUR TEAM

Of course it always makes sense to build a recipe by knowing the ingredients you will be using. What could be more certain than starting from seed? (Maybe that instinct comes courtesy of Grandma Ruth and the influence of her years down on the farm?) Your job is to select the good seeds from what is available, decide how many of each kind you need to make the right mix and then create the best conditions for them to take root.

If you are a parent, you identify what your children are good at and where they are challenged. You work to "manage" and encourage their strong skills and take steps to improve any weaknesses. It may turn out that some of the weaknesses are best just left alone. Maybe you decide to give up the singing lessons when you realize your kid cannot carry a tune.

This is the kind of thing a good teacher does as a crucial part of her job. In a school you are usually assigned your students so you need to play the hand you are dealt in a way similar to a parent. As a parent, you typically have your responsibility for life. A teacher may have the freedom to move a child to a different classroom if circumstances warrant.

If you manage adults in a corporate environment or any other kind of organization, you do well to follow the same principles as those for managing children. Here, you also may be assigned or "inherit" a crew to manage. Like the teacher, you are likely to have the liberty to make changes if necessary. Getting to know the Types and their typical characteristics will expand your powers of selecting good seeds and combining them together into a wholesome mix.

LOOK INSIDE

Your first task with an inherited group is to get to know each individual in it. It's good to start this effort right from the beginning. The way I do this is to spend time with them one by one to get a solid idea of who they are. I find that paying attention to the details of their work is the best way to assess their skills, talents and weaknesses. This is also the way to find out their quirks and special strengths and to learn about their ambitions and the career paths they are seeking.

Doing this well helps to make you smart about recruiting new members to add onto your team. When you are in a managerial role with the same group for any length of time, it is critical that you become proficient at finding talented people who will mix well with them. Those you identify need to be capable in their own right but also complementary to the folks you already have in place. If you have a lot of broccoli and potatoes, maybe it will be good to add some tomatoes and an onion.

LOOK OUTSIDE

I strongly advocate that as a manager you should take every opportunity to get to know people outside of your own group. For many years, I have made it a point to meet with anyone who asks. Think of it as networking with your co-workers or information gathering or just an opportunity to have a friendly talk about what's happening on the job.

I have informal meetings, lunches and sometimes dinners for this purpose several times a week. I do this with people who used to work for me, friends of theirs, senior people in my same or other departments or young people just starting out who may have heard it is a good idea to talk with me. I do this with people inside my firm as well as from other companies.

I have been told over and over how helpful this has been to the person seeking advice or perspective. It is especially valuable in an organization like the one I've been in for so long that has a lot of movement of people from one group to another. That's because when those moves happen, you already know the pool of people available to fill openings, whether in your own group or others. So it is always helpful to me as a manager too.

Because of the effort you made to know your people well, you will have clarity about the kind of person you want to add when the time comes to expand your team. And because you have made the effort to know who is available, filling that slot will be easier. This is not a owwme exercise but an ongoing, daily activity that will make your long-term success greater and easier. Plus, it's really interesting to get to know all those people!

INTERVIEWING

The organization where I work puts an enormous amount of effort into recruiting and interviewing. There have been many times over the years when I have thought it a little extreme. What has felt to me an excessively elaborate process could have been replaced with smarter and more focused interviews. Consensus thinking hasn't always resulted in better results.

I remember one time when we hired someone for a fairly senior role. He had wonderful credentials and was incredibly presentable and articulate. This individual interviewed for two different client-facing roles and was offered and accepted one of them. In the process, he met with at least 40 people across the global organization.

Six months after joining the firm, he was let go. The problems were mostly about the absence of substance behind his pretty façade, his "fluffing" glib talk and his "entitled" background. The question is, how could all 40 people not have picked up that there was an issue with substance? Perhaps a smaller and more focused group, with fewer approvals required, would have brought the deficiency to the surface?

In truth, you have to accept the fact that you will make mistakes in hiring. Regardless how creative you get with the interview process you can't really evaluate everything in advance. It is simply not possible to always predict things like a person's temperament, ability to manage a team or to make good judgments, based just on interviews.

Sometimes there are things you can do when interviewing that will lessen the likelihood of mis-hire. Smarter interviewing may mean adjusting your approach for different kinds of people. I will discuss interviewing in each of the chapters about the six different Types.

THE CANDIDATE

I have some general principles about interviewing that I have found very useful. The first three are about the candidate.

1. I like to delete the candidates' names and outside interests from their resumes before they are distributed to those who will interview them. I especially make sure to do this for junior positions. This helps to offset the many biases that exist. When a resume is made "anonymous" in this way, I find the evaluation is more dependably based on that person's actual experience and accomplishments.

2. I always take attitude over ability. I prefer someone who is willing to fix the hardware, empty the trash or wash the windows over anyone who wants to tell me how qualified or, worse, over-qualified he is for a position. Give me a break! People need to be hungry, respectful and un-entitled. Otherwise, I find, they usually won't work out.

3. Never close the door on any candidate unless he is a clear disaster or clueless or really doesn't share your core business beliefs or ethics. If the latter is true, you should tell him. It will help him find his way with other organizations. This has always worked for me.

THE PROCESS

The next three recommendations are about the interviewing process.

1. Decide up front who needs to be part of the interviewing process and then keep it controlled. I've learned that you do best with a small and directly relevant group of people. Five to seven interviewers is a reasonable number, although that will also be influenced by the level of the position and the need for buy-in from others in the organization.

2. Make your decision quickly, let the candidate know what it is right away and don't waver from your decision.

3. Always follow your gut. If you or the other interviewers are unsure of your decision, then you need to repeat the process.

GO LAST

Finally, I am going to disclose my confidential and long-standing interviewing secret: I intentionally manipulate the interview schedule so I can go last. At the least, I make sure my turn comes after several other people have interviewed the candidate. My technique then is to just let the candidate speak to me. I don't say much, although sometimes that is quite a challenge for me!

This technique allows me to test the knowledge of the candidate as well as her ability to remember details on the fly from the other interviews she has just had. The result is that I gain a sense of who she is and get insights into her grasp of what it is we are asking her to do. It is dependably effective and revealing.

PREPARING THE SOIL

When the new kid shows up in class or a new person joins any other kind of group, there are things a teacher or manager can do to help him or her have a smooth entry. It is generally a challenging time for the newbie, even if it's a star and even if it's someone with lots of experience. Getting the new folks started on the right foot can go a long way to ensuring success, both for them and for the team.

In addition to helping out the new person, you can use the early days of his time with you to confirm that you have made a good selection. I learned the hard way that, even with the greatest care in the interviewing process, you can still make a mistake in hiring. Working closely with the new recruit right from his first days may help you discover such a mistake quickly.

A great way to start the newcomer out is to give him a concentrated orientation to the job and the people. Convey to him your personal overview of the group and

---

its ways, coupled with explicit information about how he is expected to fit in. This can save everyone a lot of time.

I make it a point to personally take him around to meet the other team members. A side benefit of this is the clear signal your attention sends to the rest of the crew as you personally introduce him to them. This can be a big help in gaining respect for him from the rest of the team.

CULTURE

The way the new seed fits in will depend a lot on the culture of the group. I have observed the importance of this intangible in many organizations. Managing your children, a technology company, a classroom or a global collection of yoga teachers all rests on the essential glue that is the culture. Such culture can't be dictated, it has to be lived every day and no matter what the weather. It must reside in the DNA of the individuals who make up the group.

This is something that starts at the top with the leader of the organization. The values and attitudes of a CEO or President or Executive Director invariably permeate the company and define its culture. The same is true within departments and smaller units as well.

I am a huge advocate of a culture that supports the strengthening of every single member of the group, continuously helping each one to get smarter, happier and more successful. When this kind of culture is strong from bottom to top, the organization will have the natural reflex of making sure everyone is growing. That ensures that all of its members feel responsible for the long-term success of the whole. If someone on the team falters, then the others become more united and will work together to make things better. On the other hand, if the leader of a team or organization is autocratic or unable to share the responsibility for carrying out the mission, just one serious misstep by her can leave the organization in a struggle to survive.

TEACHING AND TEACHING

Strengthening all members of the group means making sure they are all learning. Remember the story of my mother and the homework at the dining room table? Learning how to teach has been a centrally important ingredient in my success. This does not mean selectively choosing top employees or students for certain exercises but being inclusive with everyone all the time. Doing this with the new people right from the start is a good way to help them fit in and to see if they have the capabilities the group needs.

Even if you are the kind of manager who believes that your employees exist solely to make you look better (now there's a twisted culture), you had best make sure that they know what it is they are supposed to do! Although I find this sort of management short sighted, it supports my belief that a focus on teaching everyone is important to both personal and overall organizational success.

The things you do to strengthen, broaden and develop children are the same things to do as a manager or a leader. Just as you encourage little Johnny to help his sister Susie, you need to offer encouragement to everyone around you, no matter if you are a hotel manager, a head chef, a line supervisor in a factory or head of a trading desk. Remember that all ships rise together and even the small boats benefit from being exposed to the high tides. You'll find the crew will be happiest when everyone rows together.

GETTING OVER "THE HUMP "

One of my favorite arrows in my quiver of management wisdom is my "hump" speech. It is always helpful to a new person joining the team and it is just as helpful every time someone undertakes something new. This speech explains that any new challenge or worthwhile endeavor is generally hard at the beginning and gets worse before it gets better. Then one day, you suddenly notice that you are feeling the groove and you realize that you have made it over "the hump."

Time and again I have seen this advice prove valuable to people who have been pushed outside of their comfort zones. It is always helpful to people who doubt that they can master something new. I like to check in with someone while he is going through this phase. For those who know me all I have to ask is, "How's the hump?" The typical outcome is that these individuals resolve to stick with the challenge, gain momentum and thrive. I *love* giving this advice!

As a manager, this is also great advice that I give myself. I need to remind myself of it when new employees, or people taking on bigger responsibilities, are going through their "hump" phase. I need to breathe, be patient and remember my responsibility to support them.

HELP ME HELP YOU

Just as I constantly make the effort to help people grow every day I also work to instill that same responsibility in everyone in the group, from the bottom to the top. I like to use the expression "help me help you." Most people love to be told to help someone else learn something that they know how to do.

It is good to position your request as an opportunity for the individual eventually to delegate the task he or she is teaching. The person doing the teaching can then look ahead to the potential of taking on something new. I think Johnny would be eager to help Susie learn how to wash the dishes so that he can move on to the new, larger responsibilities of garbage removal and bathroom cleaning!

Organizations typically refer to these efforts as "development." Think of how many times you have heard about "child development" or "professional development." Many organizations actually have a position called something like "Director of Learning and Development." Yes, it might be good to have such a department responsible for guiding people along, but getting better at what you do and making sure those around you do the same really is everyone's individual responsibility. This is that culture of strengthening I spoke about and it needs to be at the heart of every family and organization.

I am not trained in development. I became good at it simply by doing it. I tried lots of things that didn't work so well and some that have worked very well for many years. I have had the benefit of the occasional training class on this sort of thing but most of my advice to you comes straight from my own experiences. Remember, my whole career evolved not from planning but simply from being willing to "do whatever it takes," admitting what I didn't know and then figuring it out.

Now that you have identified and selected the right seeds and made sure the soil is prepared for them, you must be sure to give them nourishment.

CHAPTER 5

NOURISH THEM

NEW YORK CITY, NEW YORK. I was on my way to pick up lunch recently when I ran into a former colleague I hadn't seen for a few years. I thought how his current job and life must be very aligned with the stars because he looked better than ever, well rested and happy.

We got into a discussion about the people we used to work with and which ones we had seen when. We commented about one in particular who has had almost as many different positions as I have, only his were all at different firms and in about half the number of years. We had a few good chuckles. As we were reviewing our personal and professional adventures, I knew that we would eventually get to some memorable feedback I had once given him, which to this day makes us both laugh.

The group I was managing at the time liked to joke with me about what they called my "drive-by comments." I have always walked very quickly and I developed a habit of tossing out feedback to people as I passed their desks, without any context or explanation. This is not something I am proud of and I corrected it pretty quickly after I became the brunt of their jokes. The comment I made to this colleague as I flew by on my way to a meeting was, "I heard bad things about you." Of course it was delivered in clipped tones. Honestly, I didn't remember even then what I had heard that I described as "bad."

There is no question that feedback is best when delivered on a timely basis. But giving random feedback is just bad form. Without details or background, flyaway comments can be destructive. They are likely leave the recipient wondering exactly what was meant. It's an especially bad idea to do this publicly.

But it's an even worse idea not to give feedback at all. It surprises and dismays me how many parents, teachers and managers shy away from delivering feedback, when it is such a crucial part of communicating and managing. Children, students, soldiers, employees, even friends, all need to know how they are doing – and how are they to know if you don't tell them?

REPORT CARDS

From the time we are born, someone is assessing our progress. I'd bet most of us have a photograph someone took of the first time we stood on our own two feet. Our parents probably saved our school report cards and various other items that measured our progress though life. As we move into the adult world, we have been conditioned to expect feedback and measures of success. Why is it that we do not always receive it as adults? Why is it that we are not sure how we are doing?

I interviewed a retired army general who gave me some pretty good insight into how the military measures performance. He says it is quite similar to getting report cards when you are a student and it is carried out with the same regular discipline. These reports are critical to a soldier's career because they determine his advancement and subsequent assignments.

I am fortunate that the large company where I have spent my entire career is very disciplined about performance reviews. This firm spends tons of time with mid-year and year-end reviews. In many organizations and in parts of my own the frequency and quality of these assessments fluctuate and are pretty much dependent on the individual manager.

FEEDBACK

Feedback is the core nourishment you can offer your children, students, colleagues or any other group members. I find it especially frustrating when people come to me for advice and tell me that their manager, partner or teacher never gives them any feedback. Of course they feel clueless as to whether or not they are doing well.

Perhaps this happens because managers do not learn how to do it or do not recognize how important it is. However, I believe it is more frequently rooted in fear of confrontation and prickly situations.

I have figured out that there are several elements that make feedback really helpful. It needs to be immediate and frequent, direct and honest and well balanced. Your ability to do it well depends on really knowing the individual and the circumstances of his or her work. You accomplish this best by going "into the fields" regularly, right alongside your team, as I describe in a later chapter. I learned long ago that the more you give feedback in this fashion, the easier it becomes to deliver.

IMMEDIATE AND FREQUENT

Whenever possible, feedback should be given as close as you can to the time you notice something that warrants comment. If you are engaged alone with the individual, do it right then. Perhaps, if you are in a meeting or another group situation, you will wait until you can speak privately. Just make sure it's right away and don't put it off for another day.

As a huge believer in frequent feedback, I am known for showering my team with my comments on their work. A big benefit of this is that the more often they hear how they're doing, the less charged each bit of feedback becomes. In my groups, it was an expected part of our regular interactions.

DIRECT AND HONEST

I am also pegged as being fearless in delivering comments that are both very direct and completely honest. In my opinion, being straightforward in giving someone information about how she is doing is the best way to be sure the message gets across. The more direct your points are, the better. Misunderstandings because of lack of clarity do no one any good. This is a case where good communication skills are key.

Being fully honest in your feedback is another essential step toward helping someone develop and grow. This is imperative in order to be sure that no one is taken by surprise by decisions that affect them. Your candor is also important to the quality of the relationship, since honesty builds trust and you both know it when it happens.

Of course, I also meet with people who actually are getting feedback regularly but are in denial about what they hear. This is where their honesty with themselves is lacking and they retreat into denial. Denial can happen with all the Types, each in his own way.

WELL BALANCED

Immediate, frank, balanced feedback is the most effective tool both for reinforcing positive behavior and for correcting undesirable behavior. When I refer to balanced feedback, I mean accompanying a message about poor performance with specific suggestions about doing things differently or recommendations to learn new skills, as well as offering encouragement to improve.

Of course, if there are positive results along with disappointing ones, be sure to speak about those at the same time. Most managers are happy to give positive feedback. It makes the person receiving it happy and motivated and leaves the manager satisfied. Everyone feels good about a job well done.

Many leaders don't like to deliver critical messages but I have found that if your people really understand what you think, this practice actually strengthens your relationships with them. Often managers want to avoid giving a bad review because it makes them uncomfortable and taps into their fear of conflict. It is very tempting just to dodge what might result in an unpleasant conversation.

This is a mistake in my opinion. I see a criticism as just the opening note in a song about improvement and advancement. That's why I don't call it "negative" feedback but always use the term "constructive." When you give this kind of feedback, it's extra important to be clear and specific about what needs work and to let the individual know you are committed to helping him or her improve.

What is the most important thing about delivering positive, constructive, disappointing or tough messages?

You need to just do it! Deliver all messages. Don't pick and choose and don't put it off. Feedback needs to be done continuously, on a timely basis and not all saved up for some end of year discussion.

"THAT'S WHAT MY HUSBAND TELLS ME"

Many years ago I learned a valuable lesson about con-fronting persistent uncomfortable situations. I had joined a new team and was working with a group of people I didn't know at all. One of the people on the team seemed to have an issue with my being there. I felt like she didn't even get to know me before she started to point out facts she thought I didn't know or to make remarks about my experience, my past and even my personal life.

I wasn't practicing yoga then so I wasn't yet trained in breathing techniques and I do remember holding my breath each time she reminded me of my shortcomings. Eventually, I decided to confront her. I asked for an expla-nation for her apparent dislike of everything about me. I cited many examples.

My colleague didn't seem to be surprised at all and after some tears said, "My husband tells me that all the time." It turned out that what her husband had referred to was the disparaging way she tended to speak to waiters, shop clerks and others in service positions. After an apol-ogy, my colleague and now friend stated her commitment to working on improving her interactions with me and asked for help improving her communication with others.

After this conversation, I considered all the times I had delayed delivering the feedback necessary to correct a sit-uation. Then I stopped delaying. Of course, you get the occasional denial. But it surprised me somewhat that most of the time I heard responses from people that showed they already knew they needed to improve or change. It wasn't the first time they had heard the feedback I was giving them.

My conclusion is that they usually already know anyway, so don't delay bringing it up.

HUMOR AND ENCOURAGEMENT

When dealing with most people, I take the humor that I learned from my mother and use it to diffuse difficult situations. Lightening the tone can make the message more acceptable to some people. However, others may take offense, so it's important to really know the person you're talking with.

While being direct, I develop my message to be encouraging and constructive. Some of my best performers have told me they know that sometimes my criticism can be harsh but they also say it helps them. They accept it because they know I am well intentioned.

As you get into the habit of giving continuous feedback, it's good practice to follow up with the individual regularly to ensure that he knows you are keeping up with his progress. This is when you can acknowledge positive changes in his work. It is also very effective to look for and cite other unrelated progress that he may be making. You can't just bark without later distributing biscuits for good behavior.

KEEP CURRENT

In order to stay in touch with your crew from the bottom up, you need to check in often. Keeping up to date with their work and uncovering their concerns is the best way to see how each one is developing and what someone might need in order to find more success.

Just as I insist on keeping an eye on the progress of my team's work, I equally recommend that a good leader should keep her superiors current with her own progress. As usual, good communication is always the best policy.

GIVE ME AN UPDATE

I advise a manager or teacher to be explicit in teaching people the value of checking in when working on a project or a report. It can be frustrating to a leader to wait and wait for some sign that things are moving forward and yet hear nothing about the progress. It gets even more frustrating when you finally do get to see the progress and you realize that things have moved in a direction that was not as you intended.

You do a favor for a student, a colleague, an employee or someone's child when you teach him that it is always a good idea to give such progress updates to those who have an interest in his work. Although it may be accurate that he is working diligently on an assignment, without periodic checkpoints he could end up delivering something other than what was expected. I urge him to accept that it is much better to get regular reality checks from those who are waiting for the results of his greatness.

I often had to teach this lesson to young bucks new to my group. They would want to impress me quickly with their skills. I was usually confident in their ability to get the task done but I always urged everyone to show me their work as it progressed. I wanted to avoid having them move too far astray. Younger professionals might view these reality checks as a sign of weakness or inability to follow instructions. I have always viewed the periodic check-ins as a sign of confidence and maturity.

I would say, "Be sure to check in with me as you work through this project. Please don't wait until you have it fully baked!" Generally people would hear me the first time I gave this advice and follow it accordingly. Of course some of those young bucks would need a few reminders and some would repeatedly ignore my wishes. Then they would deliver beautiful work but something that was not really useful for my current purposes. These situations then result in costly delays.

It gets even more interesting when the wild buck wants to debate their point that what they did is actually superior to what it is you requested! This is when it can become not only frustrating but usually even more costly and inefficient as well.

ASK FOR IT

Just as it is essential for each member of your team to have individual feedback from you, it's important that you get feedback for yourself. If you are not a student or in the military, you may not be getting periodic updates on how you are doing. If that's the case, ask for them.

Clearly there are some jobs, like sales, that do it very directly and are based solely on a single metric. But if you are not a commissioned salesperson, you might find yourself seeking some feedback on your performance and also wanting advice on what you can do better. Your career progress and compensation are probably all mixed into your quality of life, self-esteem and overall happiness, so shouldn't you demand some guidance? After all, you do spend a lot of time working.

The real challenge comes in the subsequent re-evaluation of your progress and in putting focus on your ongoing development. In any people-intensive business, this is exceedingly important. In large companies these evaluations may not always seem "fair" but the discipline of the process is valuable. If you toil in a business or company that doesn't have a real framework of metrics for measuring your progress, you should speak up. As a manager, you should do this on behalf of the members of your group.

KUDOS

Let's just focus on compliments for a bit. We all need to remember to give compliments and also remember to accept them properly as well. Perhaps those of us who are uncomfortable receiving them also forget or decline to give them. Even worse is if you only speak to people when you are telling them what they did wrong.

An Asian colleague told me about her experience.

"One of the things I'm not good at, and am trying to work on, is giving and receiving compliments. On the giving side, I've always been taught to be mindful of not sounding insincere (i.e., don't be excessive). And I tend to have taken it too far, by not saying enough, which often makes people think I'm aloof and cold. Similarly, on the receiving end, as you can imagine with Asian parenting, compliments are not things I heard much growing up, and even when given, compliments usually get dismissed. And so over time, I've felt uncomfortable when caught in both the giving and receiving camp."

I think this applies to many of us, regardless of our heritage or background. I have said how it is important to communicate well and I am very strongly in favor of giving feedback. It is important as well to be able to give compliments and to accept them with an appropriate level of appreciation.

DISAGREEMENT

I frequently receive requests for advice on the merits, risks and techniques of how to disagree. This is a rich and sensitive topic that is important to parenting, teaching and managing. It is also one that has no single solution. Practiced without care, disagreement can be dangerous to the relationship of parents with children, teachers with students and managers with colleagues.

My belief is that people will and should disagree. It is natural and makes for healthy debates, thoughtful outcomes and stronger organizations. It is key to building, strengthening and deepening relationships with your family, friends, colleagues and managers. It's a good idea to say so if you have a legitimate difference of opinion.

Of course, how you practice disagreement with your manager or leader is a tricky matter, because it can make or break your accession into corporate sainthood. You will do your children, students, employees, team members and colleagues a lifelong favor by helping them learn how to express their opinion when it is contrary to the prevailing thinking.

I often hear questions from people asking, "Do I dare to disagree with my boss?" (Yes.) "Is it appropriate to use humor to disagree?" (Yes, but not sarcastic humor.) "How do I know if my manager appreciates when I disagree with her?" (Tricky. Depends on how well you know each other.) "Do I express my disagreement in a public forum or should I always do it privately?" (Keep it private at first.) "How do I control my anger when I strongly disagree?" (Breathe and save it for another day.)

TAILORING YOUR FACTS

The most important and too often forgotten point about having a disagreement is that you need to know your facts! Without them, your arguments will be weak and you may be crushed.

Meet Ricky, my custom tailor. He owns and manages his own custom clothing firm in Hong Kong. I first met Ricky many years ago when he was an employee of a well-established and well-known tailor shop. When he left to start his own company, I was quick to move my business to him, as did many of my colleagues who all were big fans of this young entrepreneur. I always like working with Ricky because he has a gift of disagreeing with almost everything I might say.

I am not an easy customer when it comes to making my suits or shirts. I think most people are somewhat picky about their clothes and think they know what looks good. I am no exception. My sartorial aggression has never bothered Ricky. He just listens, disagrees and then gives me all sorts of great reasons why I should do as he says. I usually comply and he typically gets his way. I am a very happy customer.

Ricky does not disagree just for its own sake. I have lived and worked with many people who seem to disagree with everything anyone thinks or says. These people are just annoying and counterproductive. We call them "Constant Commenters."

Ricky is different. He gathers details about my size, shape and preferences for fabrics, colors and styles. He listens to what I think, lets me know that I have gained weight and then begins to discuss and debate what I should be choosing. He incorporates his previous experience with me, the changes in my situation and his experiences with others, as well as his inventory of fabrics and colors. He then tells me why I am wrong and follows immediately with brilliant alternative suggestions.

He does all of this with facts. It works beautifully because there is a healthy balance of fact, persuasion and occasionally letting me get my way. Sometimes, Ricky just lets me do all the talking.

I know so many people who could learn so much from Ricky. Some of them could also benefit enormously from his dressing and style advice.

WHY TO DO IT

Disagreement is one of the most fruitful kinds of conversation when it's respectful and based on serious thought. I have always yearned for it in my working life because a good challenge sharpens thinking and clarifies issues. I rarely got it though, which was always a big disappointment and made me feel a bit insecure.

I had a recent example of disagreement when a friend sent a group of us an email that showed a "joke" t-shirt and admonished us to think deeply about its message because she was sure we could all agree about it. I found the message extremely offensive and decided I needed to say something. So I wrote a reply disagreeing with it and I was so interested in the two kinds of responses I received. First was an admission from the sender that she'd been a bit warped in sending it in the first place. The other was the series of thanks from several others that I'd spoken up. Oh the beauty and merits of feedback!

Disagreeing is a way of revealing yourself, which of course makes you vulnerable to judgment by others. So it takes a certain strength of character.

HOW TO DO IT

As a manager, I always encourage disagreement when it is strongly reasoned. It is important and so crucial that we learn how to do this without angering people or damaging important relationships. Expressing your own different opinion on an issue should be done with respect and, when it is done thoughtfully, it will most likely earn you respect in return.

We also all need to learn to agree to disagree. We don't always need to persuade everyone else to adopt our point of view. Sometimes there are legitimately differing judgments and the resolution lies elsewhere. Recognizing when to back away is a valuable skill too.

The grace or antagonism with which we insist on our own opinion may sometimes matter more than the substance of our actual argument. This is a case of style, where it's less important whether you win or lose but how you play game that affects the outcome. This goes directly to the ability to communicate effectively.

WHEN TO DO IT

We should all disagree periodically. I am struggling to think of a situation where it is not a good idea to express an opinion of your own that is based on your honest beliefs, experience, or understanding of the facts. We all have experienced or read about situations where the suppression of opinions has resulted in rebellion, war, divorce, drop-outs or people losing their jobs

We know that teenagers are experts at disagreement. Isn't everything a debate? Teens can be tenacious about winning their arguments and insisting on getting what they want. However, there is also a limit to the usefulness of disagreement.

When I was a teenager, if my father didn't like one of my friends he would say, "I thought you stopped mixin' with that cat." This was how my father made it clear to me that he disagreed with my judgment. At some point I remember hearing my father's objections and then deciding to just move on with my own decisions.

It is usually the case that in school or the sports team or the military, the teacher or coach or commanding officer will be the decision maker and have the last word. On the other hand, in some organizations there are times when consensus is preferable and your persuasiveness and close reasoning can make a real difference. You need to be clear about when consensus it is not desired. Then you are well advised to do as your boss has required!

MORAL COMPASS

I recently read a book in which one of the main characters is a young woman who murders men who have physically abused woman. I understand that this is wrong. I give lots of money to charities. I understand that this is right. My friend read a very long book about Lyndon Johnson that said he frequently lied to get what he wanted. This is where the fun begins.

You might think that Johnson was a politician and therefore you would expect that he would lie. But don't most people in all walks of life do things or say things that may not be exactly completely truthful in order to get some desired result?

I am not a parent but I am sure that most parents can tell me how to ensure that your young ones don't lie and how you teach them right from wrong. I grew up in a Catholic family, so lying was a big part of the quilt of guilt and confession. Our Jewish friends think about the untruths that they may have told each past year as they observe Yom Kippur. Deciding what is right or wrong is an enduring condition of life. I struggle with this often as it relates to my writing, my daily activities and relationships, how to manage people and business decisions.

As a rule, I use my gut as a guide and that has worked well for me. I think of my gut as my "moral compass" but I am very conscious of trying to not act like I live on some superior moral plane. This is not easy when you feel strongly about something. It's also difficult when you want to support someone you believe is being treated unfairly, or you want to defend an action that you really believe is the right thing to do. It gets particularly complex when you layer on large groups of decision makers, corporate politics and hidden agendas.

Then there are the people who just don't tell you the real story. I suppose it is preferable that people leave out things rather than tell you untrue things.

FRUSTRATION

I have been studying the fine art of Mindfulness. Part of this philosophy of awareness is focused on simply how to be present today, perhaps put your disappointments aside and enjoy now.

How we handle frustration is very telling. Parents and teachers have the earliest and most important role in teaching young people how to deal with outcomes that may not be the ones they hoped for. Leaders reveal a lot about their abilities and character in the way they manage disappointment, difficult situations and disagreements.

I have had my share of personal frustration. What is important for me now is my ability to be mindful of how I handle it. The more mindful I am of my thoughts and reactions, the more it seems things can appear positive and constructive.

As I often preach (but still may not always practice), we need to pause, breathe and only then move forward with decisions and actions. When I reflect on my long career, more often than not the things I remember with some regret are the instances where I was not able to manage a disappointment in a calm, mature way. Now I do much better when I listen, pause, breathe and only then mindfully respond.

MENTORING

Mentoring can play a vital part in organizations large and small,. It is important not only for an individual's growth, but vital for the success of a business, a team or any other group. If all the little ships don't rise together, the big ship won't either. I have always been surprised to find people who have the attitude, "What can you do for me?" as opposed to, "What can I do to help all of us succeed?"

Mentoring is one of the most direct ways to provide nourishment to an employee, colleague or team member. We all need to figure out a way to make mentoring relationships evolve naturally and broadly. It is imperative that support for this starts at the top of an organization and it needs to be genuine. People tend to tell others about good mentoring experiences and that is the best way to get buy-in. This is a big part of the glue of the organization's culture.

I have had the good fortune to work for a firm that does a reasonably good job of creating an environment of mentoring. There are mentoring programs, information about them on its websites and periodic mandates that every senior person sign up to participate. It is all good and much better than most corporations but I am not always so sure it is as effective as desired. Because people are so busy, the "mentoring" often can turn into just a periodic lunch date between the mentor and the mentee.

My best mentoring relationships have been those that have evolved naturally. There are several people who have been instrumental in my growth and success in this way. These were sometimes people I worked for, but not necessarily. In all cases, they were people who took a genuine interest in my development because of a shared objective or a shared interest. It was what I call "organic" mentoring.

This kind of relationship happens when the mentee also offers something needed by the mentor. An example from my own experience is the manager who asked me to take over the trading desk when he needed me to figure out how to make that business work. I, of course, wanted career advancement. Later, after I moved on to another department, that first manager still continued to help me in many ways and that extended over the entire course of my career. He long ago left the firm, yet we are still in touch.

CHAPTER 6

IRRIGATE WELL

LONDON, ENGLAND. Here in London, they speak English, the same language as the one I grew up with in Philadelphia. Except that it is not. Aside from the differences in vocabulary and in usage of seemingly similar phrases, there are fundamental and subtle cultural differences and expectations that are both a delight and a challenge.

Did you know that the word "rubber" in American English could mean rain shoes or a condom, while in England a rubber is an eraser? I remember one time early in my career when a female colleague from England was yelling that she couldn't find her "rubber." This was hilarious to me and the more so as it was more than 25 years ago, when there were almost no women in the financial industry.

I have a friend who is the CEO of a global public relations firm that specializes in luxury resorts. She told me about a time that a couple of her colleagues had asked a client in Vietnam for a "ball park figure." The client had no idea what that meant and probably wondered if they were speaking English.

Even when you know the language of the people you interact with, you still need to know so much more in order to communicate successfully. A lot of this additional knowledge comes from working closely with your people. I call this "working in the fields" and it is the subject of the next chapter. That is the way you learn the slang and your people's underlying attitudes about all sorts of things.

To be effective in the fields, the biggest requirement is that you communicate well. Good communication is the irrigation that delivers the nourishment you have to offer. Through communication with your students, children, employees or the members of any team you lead, you give the information they need to learn and grow. When you share with them, they gain from your knowledge and experience. By listening to their questions and suggestions, you can identify their needs and benefit from their ideas and contributions. It is the central skill to giving good feedback and being a good mentor.

SPEAK UP

The way we communicate is the first and most important skill that we all need to improve and develop if we wish to succeed. You can be only marginally talented but if you excel at speaking or making a compelling argument, you will do just fine.

I repeatedly advise parents and teachers to urge their young charges to become part of the drama troupe or to participate in the debate club so they can learn and master the art of communicating. I also apply this to coaches, mentors, advisors and managers of any kind of group.

I consider this one of the most helpful things a leader can do to guide young people to enlarge their life options.

To learn acting is to find your voice and competently speak publicly without fear before others. This instills confidence to speak up in a group setting and teaches you how to conduct yourself. In debate, you learn to break down a topic, analyze it and then develop and express arguments and counter-arguments. This is directly useful in problem solving and persuading others.

Repetition is one of the techniques of good communication. So I repeat: my most enthusiastic and simple recommendation to anybody is to:

- Take acting classes
- Join a debate club
- Practice, practice, practice!

I have learned that it is important to become aware of your own communication style. Once you are aware of it, you can become sensitive to its impact and then find ways to improve on it. When you have learned to recognize your own patterns and habits, you are better able to see those of others as well. That makes you a good mentor for your team members, so they can improve their communication style for their own benefit.

LISTEN, JUST SHUT UP AND SAY SOMETHING

First-rate communication skills are pre-requisite for being effective at giving feedback and mentoring. To communicate is to speak, of course. It is also to listen. In addition to the verbal, there is non-verbal communication, which telegraphs so much about our thoughts and our feelings.

A good communicator knows how to include the other person as a partner in the conversation. This means paying attention to the individual you are speaking with and making sure your thoughts are getting across. It means listening carefully to her and being open to what she has to say. This is equally true when you are addressing or participating in a group. When you can make a discussion truly interactive is when you will see the best outcome.

PLAIN TALK

The way you speak says as much about you as do the concepts you express. To get others to pay attention to your ideas, you need to communicate with them in a way that they can understand and that is believable. You can talk until you are blue in the face but if people have to struggle to understand the words you say or the expressions you keep using, you should not be surprised that they do not get your point. The point here is: speak clearly.

I insist that my team "just speak plain English or plain whatever-language-you-speak." This means to use simple words, speak in terms other people can grasp easily and avoid special lingo and acronyms. It applies to how you talk with those you teach, manage, lead, report to and with whom you conduct business. This is especially important if you work in a global organization or at a place where people speak more than one language.

I have a specific example that I give all the time: "Never use the word deck." In my mind, a "deck" is something that is built onto a house or is an open platform on a boat. I don't think of a deck as a stack of papers or series of slides that have been put together for a presentation. "Never use the word deck" means: don't use jargon.

People who use "deck" in meetings typically also want to tell you about their "deliverables," their "end-to-end" analysis," the "intellectual capital" and "reductions in force." It seems clearer to me to say, "The presentation I brought today is a thorough review of our business done by our smartest people and they are recommending that we lay off some employees."

I often tell people that they need to communicate as if they were speaking on the evening news. You want to get your message across, so it is wise to use words that people understand readily. If you think using code words, acronyms or technical terms makes you look more credible, you are mistaken. Rather than relying on such terms, make the effort to "translate" your thoughts into simple language.

As you do this, pay attention to choosing the right word to say what you mean. It can make a big difference. This is well expressed in a quote attributed to Mark Twain:

"The difference between the *almost right* word and the *right* word is really a large matter — 'tis the difference between the lightning-bug and the lightning."

As for the strange language of texting, I understand that it developed so you could write a quick message without the need to type every entire word into your palm-sized gadget. The concern I have is that texting has become the only way many adults and children communicate in writing. I wonder how many children will never fully develop their verbal and written skills and how many adults will lose theirs?

Full disclosure: I am a rabid user of both a Blackberry and an iPhone. My use of these devices is actually extreme and I am sure I have that addiction syndrome that is all over the news. I have been known to write full business plans on my Blackberry. Still, I use no truncated words, abbreviated expressions, or texting lingo. I just have really fast thumbs!

BE REAL

Even before the days of gadget-driven inattention among people, there were filler phrases. These are expressions that people repeat over and over when having a conversation. When someone does this with you, it may be intended to show interest in what you are saying but the overuse of such phrases tends to make you wonder if the person is actually paying attention or even cares what you have to say. I find it generally comes across as mindless talk. It feels insincere and makes me want to get away. I keep this topic high on my list of verbal habits that I try to avoid.

I had a conversation recently with a young colleague in London who is super bright and has a brilliant future ahead of him. (He has also developed an interest in yoga, which makes his future look even brighter to me!) I was having some sort of high-minded debate with him and I noticed, not for the first time, that he kept interjecting the expression "fair enough" after almost every statement I made.

The frequency with which he interjected "fair enough" into our conversation made me wonder, was he really agreeing with me or was he just trying to get the conversation over with so he could pursue other things? Since I am a mentor and champion of this lad and an advocate of real-time feedback, I told him my philosophy on the use of "filler expressions" and suggested he be mindful of repeatedly using expressions like this.

A few weeks later we had another telephone conversation about a totally different matter. After the conversation, the lad sent me a note asking if I had noticed that he didn't once use "fair enough" during our conversation. As they would say here in England, "Well done you! "

I generally find the repetitive use of filler expressions to imply disinterest and it even sometimes feels condescending. I have worked with many people who overuse the question, "Is that right?" as their filler. Then they make it worse when they use it with an inflection that goes up at the end. This usually tells me that they really would rather I be done with it and let them get on with their day.

Clearly the worst is when people respond to your comment or idea with the expression "Whatever" or "I have no idea." Kids and parents seem to love to make a conversation out of these phrases. Both of these expressions communicate no interest in the subject at hand and I'd venture to suggest that the speaker probably is not bothering even to consider the merits of what you have said. It is especially off-putting when hotel staff, or contractors or your employees give you these useless responses.

While there are lots of things you can say to indicate interest in a conversation, quiet listening and making eye contact are among the most effective. When someone is speaking with you, you can communicate best when you are mindful of being only in that conversation and in that moment. Being in the moment means you have less need to reassure someone of your attention by interjecting fillers.

DON'T BRO ME

How familiar do you have to be to call someone "my friend?" Is it sincere or dismissive or is it just another example of filler? I have noticed the frequent use of this expression by politicians or salespeople when they respond to questions posed by individuals. I find it condescending and I notice it is often accompanied with a cocky smirk. It always feels to me that they are really saying, "My friend, you stupid #%@!" I think it is appropriate to use "my friends" to address a crowd where there might be some actual friends in the room but people you barely know are not your friends.

This has been a pet peeve of mine for many years. In the course of my job I have managed many different trading desks and my role as leader has required me to meet with lots of trading people from external firms seeking to do business with me. These people, mostly men, tend to favor the expression "Big Guy." When they say that, I hear this: "Hey, Big Guy, what sort of crap stock can I slam on you that I know is a dog?" Please don't call me "Big Guy" and furthermore, I am not your "Buddy" either. Don't bro me if you don't know me!

There is one bright story about this. Many years ago, a young female trader worked for me at a time when there were very few female traders. One day I was enlightened about how far women on trading desks had progressed when I heard her berating someone on the telephone. "That trade you just did for me sucked and DON'T call me Girlfriend. I am not your Girlfriend! I have never even met you!"

The females of the trading tribe had identified a "Big Guy" term of their own and it was "Girlfriend." I still laugh about this because I saw it as a sign of how the trading industry was evolving by giving women opportunities to excel in a previously male-dominated profession. I suppose it was natural that they also developed their own special insincere banter.

HOW ABOUT NOT TALKING?

Let us consider that we all have two ears and one mouth. Do you think that is just some random consequence of god, genetics or evolution? Wrong! I say we have more ears than mouths because we are supposed to listen more than we speak. Just pause to think about this - and about how much you really listen.

A wise old owl lived in an oak
The more he saw the less he spoke
The less he spoke the more he heard
Why can't we all be like that wise old bird?
    —English language nursery rhyme

Listening is a skill and unfortunately too few people have mastered it. I have developed my own three-step guide to improve this part of communicating. (1) Listen. (2) Pause. (3) Then respond. What I find is that, more often than not, I do not have to respond.

Excessive talking is never a good idea. It makes you less approachable and drains energy from your listeners. I remember reading somewhere to consider three things before speaking: "Is it kind? Is it true? Is it necessary?" I think these are three great questions to consider during that pause before you respond, especially when you are dealing with difficult people, be they children, employees, colleagues or even friends. "Is it necessary?" is probably the most relevant here because it is when we talk so much that we also don't listen.

How many children do you hear say, "They just don't listen" about their parents? Of course parents say the same about their children. In organizations, many people don't even feel that they are given a forum to speak, so how can they think anyone is listening? This is why it is important for teachers, parents, coaches, managers and leaders of all kinds to create situations where everyone can both listen and be heard.

In my work place, a few of us have cards that say simply "Stop Talking." They can be convenient to hand to those people who just won't shut up. These are people who talk too much yet don't really say much, use too many words, talk over other people or don't let others finish what they have to say. Everyone should carry a few of these cards - and use them! We sometimes refer to these people as "oxygen burglars." Think how much more oxygen there would be if every one of these people talked just a little less.

There are lots of theories on why some people talk so much. It may be learned behavior from early childhood or the need to be heard if you are from a big family. Perhaps you feel yourself all-knowing and want to share your wisdom; maybe you are insecure and try to hide it behind a lot of words; or possibly you want to spare others the need to speak. I say it is just rude and insensitive, especially if you are a parent, teacher, manager or leader.

Many of us may not even realize that we are doing it. I know I wasn't aware of my "issue" until a former manager of mine made a joke about my talking. It was nice of him to bring it up 20 years later! I guess he could use some of my advice on giving timely feedback.

I had a colleague who constantly talked over me. Seriously, it was as though I were invisible. He would start talking even when I was in mid-sentence. For a long time, I tried to integrate myself into his greatness but I gave up. I got tired of it and of him and even though I gave him my feedback, nothing changed. I recognized him as the Type I call The Bully and I got myself out of the situation of having to deal with him. He continues this same behavior to this day. It seems he is a terrific salesperson but he definitely does not have a good track record with those he manages. Talk about an "oxygen burglar"! Someone should report him to the Environmental Protection Agency.

I have learned that a good way to talk less is to listen more. Here those same three steps are helpful again: listen, then pause and then respond. The pause is the challenge if you tend to talk a lot, if you assume you already know the answer or if you tend to be insecure about your part in a conversation.

It is widely known that the more fully something is thought through, the more simply it can be expressed. This is captured in another quote attributed to Mark Twain:

"If I'd had more time I'd have written a shorter letter."

If you find yourself using a lot of words to say something, you may do well to stop and figure out what it is you really want to say.

BODY TALKING

Of course you know that we all project lots of information about how we view something or someone even without talking. Our facial expressions, our posture, our physical tics and gestures all say something. They often tell a much more honest account of what we are thinking than anything we might put into words. We need both to be aware that we all communicate this way and to know how to understand it.

On one vacation I went to a spa in Arizona where a guy known as a "horse whisperer" offered a course. Before I went, I was skeptical about going to such a session because I generally thought such things suspect. Well, I took the course and it was super interesting and enlightening. (The person who teaches this course, Wyatt Webb, has an interesting book called *It's Not About The Horse*.)

The basic idea is that horses do not understand language or verbal commands; they respond to non-verbal signals. The exercises we went through were to show us how to use our body language to communicate with the horses and to get them to perform the desired behavior. It was interesting how the horse did not follow instructions when our non-verbal signals were incorrect. Clearly, there is a message in this for all of us, both personally and in our guiding of others.

NON-VERBAL SIGNALS

Are you aware of the non-verbal signals you give off? Think about your body position. Do you fold your arms when speaking to others or when sitting in meetings? That can be viewed as being defensive or having a closed mind. Do you look all around the room when you're talking with someone? That can communicate disinterest in the conversation. Do you look directly at the person you are conversing with? That tells them you are paying attention. Do you multi-task at your desk when someone is speaking to you? That can make you seem uninterested and bored. Do you stop what else you are doing when someone speaks to you? You might want to notice that.

Think about your facial expressions. Are you someone who tends to be overly expressive with your facial muscles? Do you habitually frown and maybe not even realize you are doing it? I remember many years ago someone telling me that I had looked disinterested at a very important meeting. I didn't think that I was disinterested but perhaps at some level it was true. I may just have been tired or perhaps my expression was telling the honest things that I was thinking but regardless, I was conveying something negative. I have always remembered this feedback because it was so important.

INVISIBLE WALL

Another time, also many years ago, a young colleague told me he believed my tendency to have off-putting facial expressions was the reason I don't date. About 10 years ago, I attended a weeklong silent meditation retreat where you stay in a room for 12 hours per day with 30 strangers and nobody speaks. At the end of the week, one of the participants mentioned that she didn't even notice I was in the room until the last day. She told me she could feel an invisible wall around me that indicated to her that I didn't want anyone to approach me.

Within the last year, I went to a yoga center and met some wonderful people who are now my friends. One of these individuals told me that while riding to the resort via taxi, ferry and golf cart, she kept thinking that I certainly would not be friendly or participate willingly in the group activities. It made me wonder just how many great opportunities, promotions and even dates I missed out on because people just assumed I wouldn't be interested in what they had in mind.

I put all this feedback together and resolved to learn to make connections more immediately. I want to avoid missing the opportunity to meet new people, especially as I move into the next part of my life. I also think it's wrong to deprive people of getting to know me because I am actually pretty amusing and a generally fun person!

Think about how you feel when you are speaking to others in a conversation or when speaking to a group. Are people slouched in their seats, arms folded, doodling, yawning? If you yourself do these things, are you saying you're bored and wish the talk were over with? The worst is when people text or type wildly on their Blackberries. The best is having interested faces focused on you.

See if you can notice what you are saying when you are not saying anything at all. Don't slouch, frown, doodle, fold your arms, sigh heavily or fiddle with a gadget. Smiling is always a good idea, as long as it is not some dumb, silly grin!

EYE CONTACT

Do you want my attention? Just look at me!

Do you make eye contact when you meet people? When you are speaking with someone? When you are listening to someone else speak? Many people do not and that is not the best of habits. Eye contact is a powerful form of non-verbal communication. It says you are confident, interested and present in the moment.

I find that I am suspect of people who can't look at me when they speak. It gives me a sense of distrust of them. I also find myself distracted by their lack of eye contact and therefore often miss what they are saying. I realize that it can be a symptom of deep-rooted insecurity for some or a culturally based behavior for others. Still, I always notice it and find that it limits my sense of connection to them. Check yourself. Do you make eye contact with your parents, children, students, employees, friends and pets?

I remember the time I brought my very young nephew to my office. I introduced him to many people and someone observed that he was very skillful at making eye contact. When my sister tells me of his occasional academic struggles I don't worry much because I figure that if this kid can make good eye contact with strangers, then he has the potential to communicate confidence and show he has presence. With that, he will do just fine in the world.

Now you have the right mix of seeds, you have nourished them with feedback and mentoring and irrigated them with clear and direct communication. It's time to get to work in the fields.

CHAPTER 7

WORK IN THE FIELDS

ST. ELIZABETH, JAMAICA. I am in Jamaica for a long weekend attending a yoga retreat. Most of my vacations and holidays now involve some sort of yoga and meditation activity. A yoga retreat is typically a week at a pleasant resort where the participants spend most days learning about their practice with a yoga teacher who has also traveled to the resort specifically to conduct the workshop. This one is a bohemian-hippie sort of place suitable for a gathering of yogis and yoginis.

I used to go on cycling vacations and then about eight years ago I turned in this new direction. Eight years ago, I suffered from severe chronic pain in my groin and lower back. To remedy this constant pain, I consulted every possible specialist in New York City. I took painkillers, had physical therapy, endured cortisone shots in my spine and even considered surgery. Each specialist had a different assessment of my problem and, of course, each was completely confident in his or her own solution.

Happily, I listened to none of them. Instead, I started practicing yoga. I began by going to yoga classes in my rural, weekend community. The yoga teacher there paid close attention and saw my struggles with the pain. She suggested that I consider some private lessons to get past the most difficult hurdles. She said, "I can fix you." And she did. I now practice yoga almost every day.

Just as my yoga teacher figured out my problem by working closely with me, I have found that paying close attention to the people I manage is essential. Leading a group from the ground up – really knowing the particulars of whatever it is each person does – is the best way to successfully guide and retain talented people. This practice of "working in the fields" it is at the core of my management philosophy.

So many people in management positions just don't get this, yet they "lead" packs of people in big organizations! There are some people you lead who would prefer that you went back into your office but that is important information too. It is information you won't get if you don't get close to your people and the details of their work.

FOSTERING YOUR PEOPLE

If you are over the age of 30, you may not be familiar with the pop-rock band called "Foster The People." Well, I am well over 30, I have their music and I play it frequently on my iPod and iPhone. How does someone stay close to popular culture at such an advanced age? In my case, this happens because of my regular interactions with the people I manage. It isn't just pop music I get from them but all sorts of information that helps me understand what makes them tick. It all provides me with important information for managing a business.

This could apply to a teacher or a parent or a fire chief. Staying close to those who rely on you for guidance, leadership or parenting doesn't just mean sitting in an office, having family meetings or delegating your responsibilities to another. It means taking an interest in everyone at every level, regardless of their contributions or degree of competence. If they are part of the team, class, or family, you need to stay close in order to really know what is going on with them. How else can you lead, make changes, celebrate successes and encourage growth? High-level reporting, periodic update meetings or Blackberry-focused drive-by visits just won't do it.

To foster someone is to work closely to help him or her develop. There are no shortcuts for this. You need to do it yourself. This is the single most important factor that will make you successful and respected. These direct relationships are the lifeblood of your managing efforts. If you follow this guidance consistently, it will make managing and recruiting great people almost natural and even pretty easy.

BOTTOMS UP

I am not sure where I developed this approach of managing from the bottom up. Occasionally, I have wondered if I would have been better off in the short term sometimes "managing up," a term that basically means attending more to your superiors than to those who report to you. This is sometimes also known as "sucking up." However, I have been unwilling to change what feels natural and so far that has been beneficial to me and to those around me.

I believe my connection to my people is unique because I work in the fields regularly. My philosophy of paying attention to the details (and my crazy-scary memory) means I can walk into an office I seldom visit and be able to comment on who has a new hair style, who moved to a new office and who oversaw a successful new product launch. I always get feedback that these individuals are stunned to realize I remember them and they always feel special. It is a retention tool that I believe is more effective than any corporate program designed to make people feel loyal.

Many people, in any industry, who have global roles similar to mine, leave their home base to visit company offices around the world. Most of them choose to mingle and meet with other senior people. My choice is always to sit and visit with the secretaries and junior talent. I also buy them lunch and gifts.

There is a regional cultural element to this, especially when it comes to food. Some of my colleagues might buy McDonalds for the team whether they are in Hong Kong, Houston, Madrid or Mexico City. I see how that has its charms but when you work for a global firm that happens to be headquartered in the U.S., perhaps it is better to show some sensitivity to the importance of the local environment.

For example, in Hong Kong I like to ask a local colleague to give me access to her fancy and very private dumpling club. I get heaps of dumplings and other local favorites delivered to everyone in the office – and not just those who work on my team. They are all so grateful. When in Singapore, I buy traditional Singaporain breakfast items, which the locals love but rarely eat. The residual benefit of sharing and being locally sensitive is that in the future, when you are looking for some good people, they have already looked for you! The connections you make informally through actions like this are invaluable. The more you do it, the deeper they become.

Perhaps a former team member of mine best explains my philosophy.

"I think you are successful because you make a concerted effort to get to know the people who work for you. You express genuine interest in the person and their life and you are also forthcoming with certain parts of your life. It makes people believe that you care about them and that you trust them. When people believe that you trust them, it creates a mutual respect that makes people work much harder and care much more than they normally would."

Those strong bonds help a lot when you need to identify and recruit people to join your organization or your team. I believe that my focus on managing teams and individuals from the bottom up affords me the huge benefit of having a great pipeline of willing talent who reach out to me for new opportunities. My reputation as open and inclusive gives me the ability to attract the best people. Word "on the street" is that I am tough but fair and very interested in each person's development.

TEAMWORK

Success is all about teamwork. The parent, teacher, coach, band director, scout leader or club president who can put together a smoothly running team will find her work more rewarding and the outcomes better.

The people who make the most effective leaders take pleasure and genuine satisfaction in the achievements of those around them. To them, meaningful success is collective success. These leaders are smart about putting people together to make a thriving unit. They become good at recognizing the Types and understanding how one interacts with another. They are good at mixing personalities and skill sets and they are creative about the composition of their group.

A strong leader encourages all the members of the crew to develop into team players, from the most junior to the most senior. He knows how to pair coworkers to collaborate. Such a skilled leader motivates the members to depend on each other and build trust. He understands that when the team dynamics are humming, everyone becomes more productive. He knows the benefits of team-work and draws on it to spur great achievements. In doing this, he finds personal happiness in the success of the team and the larger organization.

FACE TIME

Many months ago, I was listening to a radio interview with someone who was going on about the dysfunctional U.S. Government. Typically, I would change the station because what new could come out of such an interview? Well, this learned individual was citing the fact that the U.S. Congress only spends three days per week in Washington. She also noted that they take tons of recesses and spend loads of time campaigning. When they are in Washington, we all know that they generally just hang in their packs on opposite sides of the aisle.

Her point was that since these people barely even know each other, how can we expect them to ever get anything done? The best quote of the interview was, "Familiarity breeds attempt!" Not only did I think this very clever and accurate but also a good argument in favor of the need for "face time."

Very early in my career, I became intolerant of all the unproductive time spent making sure to be in front of the right people. Sometimes this was a matter of sticking around for long hours in order to be seen. Even worse was

Son of A Postman

sitting in endless meetings packed with people who have no real need to be there. It seems the larger and more complex a firm becomes, the more frequent these meetings, the more people who attend them and the more you sit and think of all the shareholder value that is wasted. Of course, this doesn't happen just in the corporate world but also in education, non-profits and government.

To me, it was obvious that face time was wasted time. I thought spending time in meetings or posing as a busy worker instead of actually accomplishing work was inefficient and not so smart. I would say that talking about something is an important way to get it right, but it is no substitute for actually doing it. I felt, and still do, that delivering results is the point, not face time.

Nevertheless, as I've seasoned, I've come to see that face time can be important, especially early in your career. Later on, after you have established yourself, it can feel frustrating. But let's remember that "later on" you are the more senior individual to whom the early-career person needs to have exposure. This kind of exposure is one of the important ways that knowledge, values and culture are passed along.

WORK-LIFE INTEGRATION

Because of my aversion to people who liked to "suck up" and to those who were blatantly "in my face," I was always good at spotting people who wasted time during the day. I wanted to insure productivity across the team and to lessen the need for people to hang around unproductively late into the night. I was also pretty sensitive to colleagues who are parents and their need to see their children during the week. I would regularly push people out the door to ensure we all tended to the non-work parts of our lives.

I consider it essential that organizations be aware of how much their employees feel the need to put in a big number of extended hours. If the amounts are institutionally excessive, it's time to take steps to remedy it. The problem could cause employee retention problems, which long term will just hamper the overall success of the organization.

It is important to remember that there is a cultural element to the amount of face time that may be expected. It may be more common in certain industries, like financial and legal. There are also parts of the world where it is more expected. For example, in parts of Asia it is widely practiced. In Japan, a wife would think her husband unsuccessful if he came home from the office too early. I remember a story in Korea about how the leader of a Seoul-based company told me how, if he would go into the office on a Saturday perhaps just to tend to some personal matters, everyone in the office would "miraculously" show up.

WHATEVER IT TAKES

Near the start of my career, I received some valuable advice from someone very senior in my organization. It is something that I have never forgotten and is advice I often give to others.

I was about 23 years old and had been out of college for just a short time. Here I was working in this prestigious organization full of people doing what I viewed as complicated and important business. Late one night, I was the only person left on what was a very large, open floor filled with traditional "roll-top" desks. (The use of cubicles had not yet reached this esteemed organization. Actually, I doubt anyone even evaluated office space on a cost-per-square-foot basis at that time but maybe there was someone calculating aura-and-prestige-per-square-foot!) It was 1982, well before computers had become a common desktop appliance, and I was working late into the evening on a client presentation spreadsheet, all done manually with a calculator.

That night, the top person in the company was also in the building late. He came up to me, smoking a cigarette, and asked if I knew where to locate some information. Frankly, I had no idea but I admitted that I didn't know and offered to help. Basically, my attitude to "do whatever it takes" kicked in. After I located what he needed, I whipped up a few summary statistics for him. Later that evening, the smokin' leader came back to my desk to thank me and give me this advice, "Son, in this business and in most of life, you really don't need to know much. You just need to know where to find things."

If you follow the principle of being willing to "do whatever it takes" to find things and couple it with the confidence to say, "I don't know but I will look," that will be all you need to ensure your own strengthening and development. The rest will come naturally.

"I DON'T KNOW"

I sincerely believe that it is essential for children, students, employees, friends, partners, bosses, me and everyone else to say, "I don't know" when it is true. It is always worse when you try to fake it. It is much worse when you delay progress because you really don't know how to do something or you just don't know the answer and won't admit it. Some people are skilled liars or spinners but eventually they get exposed.

This is really good advice to give to younger or more junior people because they may think it is a sign of weakness to admit they don't know something. They should learn that it is okay to say, "I don't know," followed by, "but let me find out."

A colleague who used to be in my group told me his memory of one of the first times he had to work on something for me. He said I had asked him a question to which he didn't know the answer. Instead of admitting that, he tried to come up with some convoluted response. He said he could tell I knew immediately what was happening by the nonverbal feedback of my body language. He watched my eyebrows dance up and down like they had a life of their own and realized he had to come clean. He told me it was the last time he ever did that.

SEASONINGS

In my experience, the best managers have lots of tools at hand, which gives them a big range of responses to the particular needs of their team. I have always done my best to be this kind of leader. I believe in giving guidelines and rules, encouragement and advice and generally keeping the whole of myself available to the demands of any specific situation. Often, this can lead to strong and rewarding relationships. My yoga practice and the emphasis on being mindful in the present moment, has definitely helped me in this.

I like to think of each of the following bits of advice as sprinkles of seasonings that can help add a savory flavor to the work experience.

WORKING TWO CAESARS

Many friends develop code words that they use to communicate with each other. I have found that whole vocabularies can arise between long-term friends. I have a fully developed language that I use with one friend in particular. When we are speaking in the company of others, it can drive people crazy! (I don't recommend doing this when you're managing.) With another friend, I have a particularly amusing expression we use often, "Working Two Caesars."

This friend was in a restaurant once where a prissy male waiter was feeling overwhelmed by the pressure of the patrons' demands. When one customer asked for the bill, the exasperated waiter huffed, "I can't right now! Can't you see that I'm working two Caesars?" I laugh out loud when I think of this. "Working Two Caesars" has become the expression my friend and I use to mean that we are very, very busy, doing two or more projects at once.

This brings me to think about what it is that enables some people to easily manage "Working Two Caesars," while others struggle just to get one thing accomplished at a time. Is it part of our genetic make up, something learned by example or something we can learn from a course or a book? I am no behavioral scientist, but I would argue that it is some combination of the first two. While I do believe you can learn to be organized, I think it is tough to "learn" a work ethic without a strong role model or a natural desire to achieve.

People are complex, with diverse and simultaneous needs that often have to be addressed all at once. This makes managing, teaching and leading a multi-dimensional endeavor. If you are unable to spin a few plates at once, you ought to stick to being a super-producer and let others do the managing.

THE RULE OF THREES

I believe that most things in life can be done in threes. Do you think it is just coincidence that there are three little pigs, three bears, three blind mice or three outs in a baseball game? Or perhaps this has something to do with my Catholic upbringing and that Trinity thing? The use of threes is ubiquitous. It is also easy to remember three things.

I use my "rule of threes" as a way to teach others how to get their point across clearly and in a fashion that is memorable. People who have worked for me know not to approach me with slides that have more than three important points. I know that you just lose people if you try to communicate more ideas than that. If you have five, I bet two of those five are directly related to the truly important three key points.

I enjoy the challenge of getting people to choose only three important parts to an argument or three goals for the next several months or just three bullet points on each page of a presentation. Do you know how difficult it can be to get your message clearly conveyed when you are limited to three points? It may be more difficult, but I am sure those who count will remember it better.

GLASSES WHEN YOU DON'T NEED THEM

If you are a research scientist or a tenured professor with a great level of security, please skip this section, as this is a discussion of the importance of your personal appearance. We all like to think that we are not superficial and are beyond making judgments based on appearances but the truth is that we do it all the time. We all know how important a well-groomed appearance is when interviewing for most jobs but it is also important in other aspects of life.

Recently, I interviewed a talented person in London who was very qualified for an open, client-facing position with my financial services firm. The lad came to the interview with an unshaven look, which I found distracting and probably detracted from the amount of information I absorbed from the interview. This look may work in a nightclub setting. But for this job interview? I did not think so. When I travel around the world visiting offices, I always check for the clean shavers. In other lines of work, like the arts or digital technology, this may not be the norm and certainly religious beliefs may be a reason some men choose to remain unshaven. Otherwise, it is important to be aware of what is appropriate and consider if your look is right for the position.

A major designer in the fashion business told me he knows that he doesn't save lives or cure disease but he gives prescriptions and medicine for bad taste! Perhaps we all need to give this some thought when we wear some age-inappropriate item to our workplace?

I worked for someone who frequently guided young people to wear eyeglasses, even if they didn't need them, in order to look older. I used to think this was a shallow and stupid instruction. I eventually realized how important it is to appear mature and knowledgeable in a position that requires you to serve clients personally. Call it shallow and claim you don't care, but it can help get others past some early, unfounded perceptions so they can appreciate and marvel at your brilliance.

Attention to your appearance is like all things in life: you need a good role model. Hopefully, this starts at home when you are very young and continues throughout your life. I see it as a simple expression of respect for others. I also feel better myself when I feel that I look good. I realize that I still need to perform at or above expectations, but at least I am starting from a good base.

THE LOST ARTS: ACTUALLY SPEAKING, PHYSICALLY MEETING

Something is not yet completed that you expected to have been finished long ago. You have been waiting for your child, your colleague or your employee to get it done. You inquire as to the reason for the delay.

The response is, "We are waiting on someone else."

"Why?" you ask.

"We haven't received a reply from the other party."

"Reply?"

"Yes, I sent her many e-mails but she hasn't answered."

Aarrgghh!

How about some revolutionary action steps? Did you ask her for an update when you saw her today at school? Did you get up out of your cubicle and walk across the floor or even go to another floor to ask her for some news? See that desktop instrument with buttons? It is a telephone. Pick it up and call! Then you can have a conversation about it.

We live in a device-driven world where we all know that communication is super fast. We should also be aware that lots of messages are getting lost, delayed or misinterpreted when we use only electronic gadgets to communicate. A basic skill set is in danger of becoming obsolete: talking. We need to leverage the devices but not to replace personal contact completely.

One recent Christmas, I bought all of my nieces and nephews "devices." At first I got praised for being so generous but then I got some grief for triggering the kids' growing addiction to them. What I have found as my redemption is Skype. The whole family now is very connected and they are not communicating by typing but primarily by talking with each other using this technology. This gives me hope. I have several nieces who live a long distance from each other but they are now in constant contact with each other over their live video connections. I think this is a good thing.

I also hear from colleagues that when they travel they use these tools for daily communication with their children. I even had a colleague tell me that her young son is really happy when Mommy travels now, so that he can speak to her frequently through his computer.

And you thought this was going to be a lecture to stop using devices! Please just don't use them in class, at dinner or when someone is standing in front of you speaking. And don't blame them for not closing the communication loop.

MINDFULNESS

While increasing my practice of mindfulness, I attended a conference where I was struck by a dramatically refreshing experience of meetings. At the start of each day, as participants dribbled in, everyone was asked to be silent in the hall. Some people actually participated in a guided meditation. Others just took their seats and respected the quiet time. Throughout the day, there were short pauses when we were asked to spend a few minutes breathing and contemplating the important things that we had heard.

Probably two thirds of the participants were die-hard techies with serious addictions to gadgets. Yet there were very few people using them during the presentations. This all happened naturally and without any request to refrain from using devices. People were truly listening.

Contrast this to typical company meetings where everyone rushes in and multiple warnings have to be given to shut down electronic devices. Then the stress starts and you feel the pressure build as many people are still busily preparing for their part in the day's activities. They don't take information in because they are preoccupied with what they have to put out. Discussions get off topic. The schedule gets way behind and needed breaks are canceled. Are people breathing? How much does anyone even remember what was said?

The conference I attended was well prepared and tightly choreographed. The breathing breaks gave you time to absorb what you heard. Short silent pauses helped people get refreshed and ready to pay attention to the next topic. The sessions were used for presenting work for discussion, not for preparing a talk. Gadgets were kept off out of respect for the speaker, whether she was on a dais in a large hall or a colleague sitting across a table.

I consider these to be practices that would make the workplace vastly more productive, not to mention more pleasant.

TELLING SECRETS

My presentation style was described by one of my junior people as "telling secrets." I wouldn't say that I tell people secrets but I do have an honest, direct style when speaking to a group of people. I tend not to be theoretical and I pepper everything with true anecdotes of things that have really happened, preferably ones that are entertaining. I hope this book feels like I am telling you secrets.

And speaking of secrets, be super mindful that information travels very, very quickly. Leaders, managers and even parents need to remember that all our personal electronic devices enable news to move at rapid speeds these days. This can lead to problems but it makes everything easier when you make your own best efforts to keep people in the loop. Usually it is best for your crew to hear news directly from you

KEEP PEOPLE GUESSING

When I visit offices around the world, I try to be discreet about my plans so that people will be "natural." I have adopted a policy of not telling people I am coming for a visit until the morning of my arrival. You would be surprised how well this works and I urge you to try it, even if it seems odd at first. In many places around the world, people go to work each day dressed rather casually, which is fully appropriate for many functions and may be the cultural norm. What I found is that if I announced my visits in advance, people would come to the office looking like they were on their way to a wedding or perhaps Easter Sunday church services. They always looked uncomfortable.

One time, on an office visit in the U.S., I got right up to the front door when one of the people on the team, who was out in the parking lot for some reason, spotted me. As I entered the office, I noticed some last minute scrambling and straightening throughout the open floor. I loved it!

I always find interacting with people directly and in their "normal" environment is the most reliable and efficient way to find out what is really going on and what is needed. I really enjoy walking randomly around the office chatting with everyone and getting the raw, real and valuable information.

People get bored if you don't mix things up, push them a little harder or get them to think differently. As a leader you need to refresh, come up with new ideas, new acts and fresh messages. Change is good and after normal resistance people generally embrace thoughtful and meaningful change. Of course, regardless of what you are trying to achieve, you need a plan and you need to manage that plan. But it is critical that the plan lives, breathes and gets reset to reality often.

As a manager, teacher or parent, you are also responsible for making sure people get breaks from their work. Most people around the world are surprised to learn how little time off American and some Asian workers receive. Time away from any activity, work or play, only makes it all the more special when you return. It also improves your perspective and increases your energy, your productivity and your overall satisfaction with your role in life.

DISTRACTIONS

There are some behaviors that I see in meetings and other public places that need special mention. These are things that serve as big distractions from the work at hand, whatever it may be. They have fueled two of my most well known rules: No Highlighters! No gum! They also spill over into matters of basic good manners and grappling with the issue of electronic devices.

HIGHLIGHTERS

Have you ever noticed that people who use highlighters on handouts at meetings tend to highlight almost everything on a page? Even when I was in college, I just didn't get the use of highlighters. How can you pay attention to the teacher or speaker when you are busy drawing neon lines on your page? Perhaps highlighters should only be permitted in the privacy of your bedroom? Please pay attention!

GUM

People who chew gum can be serious about their chewing. I find it a pretty unattractive habit, especially when the chewer has a particularly aggressive chew. Chewing gum is just plain annoying in a meeting. It distracts from the speaker. Please just listen!

We have a family story about the time my maternal grandmother was lying on her sofa in her living room during her last days. My mother was sitting with her. In her weakened state, Grandma abruptly sat up, turned, and looked at my mother. She said, "Katie, would you stop clacking that gum!" We believe it was the last thing she ever said. Perhaps the gum chewing was distracting her from dying?

I have recently been made aware of a study related to this important topic that has made me soften my objection. It was reported in the U.K. newspaper *Daily Mail*.

"Chomping away boosts thinking and alertness and the study reveals reaction times among chewers are up to 10 per cent faster. . . .The Japanese research published in the journal *Brain and Cognition* suggests as many as eight areas of the brain are affected by the simple act of chewing. One theory to explain the greater performance is that chewing increases arousal and leads to temporary improvements in blood flow to the brain."

Both of my sisters are elementary school teachers and when I shared the findings of this study with them, neither was surprised. They told me that it is widely practiced that students are given chewing gum when taking state standardized tests. They use peppermint gum and it is given to students starting at third grade. (I wonder why peppermint?)

This does change my opinion somewhat but I maintain that if you are going to chew, then do it quietly.

PUBLIC EATING

Related to the gum chewing is the matter of public eating. If you sit in an open floor plan and eat at your workspace, you should consider the decibel level of the food you eat. The consumption of noisy foods such as carrots and croutons can be extremely distracting.

I once had a colleague who waited each day for her desk partner to buy his lunch as her signal that it was time for her to leave the desk. She had to get away to avoid the marching band sounds of this guy's munching.

TURN IT OFF, PUT IT AWAY

I refer to the use of electronic gadgets and I consider this to be valuable advice. I don't claim to be perfect at abstaining from the ultimate in rudeness but I am aware of doing it and I do try really hard to stop it.

I remember the very early days of Blackberries. I was in a meeting with several people who were in my office making a presentation to my colleagues and me. We were the clients of this crew, yet they spent the whole meeting communicating with each other via their devices! These people used a combination of texting and non-verbal gestures to each other. It was then that I knew we were headed into a new and less sensitive world.

There is no need for me to tell you how things are today with our children, students, friends, colleagues, employees and partners all using these devices. People don't just think, they type. Often they don't listen or even appear to be paying attention. There are now studies that show that the constant use of these devices is having the same observable effect on the brain as any other addiction.

I have had a rule for many years that people in my meetings may not use their devices at all. I chide people when they whip out their chosen gadget. At the firm where I work, mobile devices are collected at all important large meetings and compliance with this policy is monitored at the beginning of each session. I think it is a prudent policy.

The worst is when you are in a one-on-one conversation with someone and he is reading or typing on his device. I have been just as guilty of this as anyone and I am really trying never to do it again.

It is interesting what is acceptable as you travel around the world. In Europe, it seems like people sit in meetings and all just go to town on their devices. In Asia and the U.S., it feels like the message that this is just plain rude is starting to get through. Turn it off. Put it away. What is so important anyway?

BOX BREAKING

One of my least favorite expressions is, "Because that is the way we do it."

Aarrgghh!

Expressions like this really mean that people refuse to change, are lazy or just not creative.

A few years ago, I was asked to manage a business that I knew very little about. As I got started, the people involved frequently told me that I knew nothing and that they already had their way of doing things. My reply to people who rely on the way things were done in the past is simple, "Don't give me that crap!"

We all need to "think outside of the box." Life is boring otherwise and frankly, people and organizations stagnate when the status quo is so rigidly revered. I say start out every day with a fresh pair of eyes. Look for a new perspective. Don't react or act or plan in the same way every day. Mix it all up. It truly does make everything so much more exciting.

To some extent, this is an attitude. As a teacher, manager or leader it is your responsibility to foster an open and creative environment regardless whether it is about how to tie shoelaces or launch a new product.

I would probably be a Postman today if I hadn't learned to think broadly. Now, now, there is nothing wrong with being a Postman but I am happy I did explore other possibilities those many years ago, as were my wonderfully supportive parents.

Speaking of moving outside of the box: One outcome of working in the fields and interacting closely with your people is that you sometimes discover tricky issues and difficult situations. The open communication helps to let problems surface. Sometimes these can be quite demanding. It's time to learn how to take action to solve them.

CHAPTER 8

WEED THEM OUT

HONG KONG, CHINA. I always like to wish my Chinese friends a happy Chinese New Year. As I write this, it is the Year of the Snake. For so long my use of the word snake has been primarily associated with a few objectionable people. Just as everyone was celebrating the start of this New Year, I went and did some research on why a person can be considered a "snake."

Here's the meaning of the snake in the Chinese calendar.

"According to one mythical legend, there is a reason for the order of the 12 animals in the 12 year cycle. The story goes that a race was held to cross a great river, and the order of the animals in the cycle was based upon their order in finishing the race. In this story, the snake compensated for not being the best swimmer by hitching a hidden ride on the

horse's hoof, and when the horse was just about to cross the finish line, jumping out, scaring the horse, and thus edging it out for sixth place."
—Wikipedia

Well, this explains a lot. I don't prefer to write negative things but it is likely you'll find yourself working with people who have snake-like tendencies at some point, unfortunate though that is. You know the kind. He takes credit for your work, steals your thoughts and articulates them as his own at meetings. You may have encountered a fellow student who wants to copy your homework just before it is due. Here's a good definition.

"A snake is someone who you think is sincere and really nice, but then turns out to be a backstabber. Someone who acts like your best friend, but who actually is the opposite."
—Urbandictionary.com

I have a pretty good ability to identify snakes and other challenged souls. You could call it a "gut instinct." I trust my gut but I also insist on having an educated gut because I do believe we must stay open to differences. We must not rush to judge someone harshly because of our own unfamiliarity with their culture or their style.

Getting your gut educated comes in part from learning how to discern what I call the Types, which you'll find later in this book. In fact, several of the Types can exhibit snake-like qualities. They can be present in a Bully, a Fluffer, an Underperformer, a Lone Ranger and have a huge sense of being Entitled. The granddaddy of snakes, though, is someone who turns out to be altogether unmanageable.

COME ON ANNIE OAKLEY!

I remember one yoga holiday in Bangalore, India, at an exceptionally well-run ashram hotel. It was punctuated by the arrival of two guests who were very loud-mouthed American women. I could tell from the moment I met them in a yoga class that their aggressive demeanor was going to lead to trouble. They were just not suited to a place like an ashram.

Well, sure enough, two days after they left, I received an email from one of the women. She was hurling all kinds of accusations at the employees of this gracious and well-run establishment. She wrote, "My necklace was stolen" and "My vacation is now marred." She was threatening to go online to mar the reputation of the entire place!

Stolen? I had total confidence that was not the case. These employees live "on campus" with their spouses and children. The majority of them have been there since the place first opened. I thought, come on Annie Oakley, put down the gun! These people would lose their livelihoods if there were even a suspicion of one of them stealing.

I felt like I was right in the middle of a big injustice. I paused and breathed and remembered the reason why I chose to come here. As I did, I noticed the great lengths being taken by the hotel staff to hunt for the missing necklace. The rooms were searched thoroughly. Furniture was even moved outside. Their top priority was to find the jewelry.

The lost (not stolen) necklace was found just a few hours later that day and returned to the Pushy American Broad whose first reaction had been to make an accusation. I continued on with a delightful stay at this enchanting guesthouse with an even higher opinion of the people who make it run so well.

UNMANAGEABLE

The story of the ashram and the necklace is an example of what happens with people who are simply unmanageable. In school and other groups, this kind of person is the troublemaker. He likes to complain, loudly, about the dumb teacher, the boring class, the stupid assignment. She's the one talking instead of listening. They make use of a technique long favored by children in an effort to get their way: If Mom says no, go ask Dad. These people adopt a negative attitude about most things and are always a very difficult challenge for parents, teachers, coaches, managers and other leaders, as well as for their siblings, peers and friends.

Unmanageable people may have a distorted idea of who they need to be to get ahead or have a self image that is derived from a fantasy. The illusion they live with overpowers the facts of their actual abilities and performance. This means there may be very little to work with in trying to help such an employee to develop and strengthen. They are unique in being essentially impossible to guide.

I have encountered unmanageable individuals as my manager, as colleagues and as those I had to manage. Almost all of these people have had many other roles since I worked with them. Some have continued to do the things they didn't do well when I was with them and still don't do them well. Some have found a way to succeed at those things they struggled with when they were with me. Others continue to bounce from role to role or company to company. Some have gone on to be successful in other industries.

In the end, I follow my own abiding preference for attitude over ability. If the candidate shows a willingness to "do whatever it takes" to get the job done and is genuinely respectful of the opportunity at hand, maybe you can take a chance. If not, remember, life is short.

CAN YOU TELL IN ADVANCE?

The very tricky thing about someone like this is that it can be nearly impossible to tell in advance who may turn out to be unmanageable. You may pick up signs in an interview process but such people are often skillful in that setting. Sometimes, you are tipped off by a blatantly pushy or self-important personality. Then you need to have a frank discussion with others who know the candidate.

What's hard to know is whether you will be able to work with her to change the behaviors. The main exception is when her negativity is so pronounced that it shows through even when she is using her best behavior to try to make a good impression in the interview. Sometimes, frankly, it just comes down to a gut feeling. This is where I especially like to have my team very involved in the interview process, so I can have the benefit of their instincts about the candidate.

Once they're on the job, you may recognize the characteristics of unmanageables as people who tend to:

- Immediately blame others when things go badly.
- Generally have a grand sense of self importance.
- Be dedicated to their own interests, usually at the expense of others.

One prominent tactic of people like this is manipulative behavior. They may try to push you into a corner to get what they want. Back-stabbing and subverting their peers and their manager is a common maneuver. They will unashamedly seek alliances with others to further their campaign against you and the team. They can be openly contentious and are unconstrained in escalating their cause for their own purposes. Sometimes they just ignore others in pursuit of their own welfare. This is not a team player.

LIFE IS SHORT

I have found that the best way to handle someone like this in the workplace is to manage him out of the group. Life is short and spending your time trying to make a hopeless situation work is futile.

The most important thing is being able to recognize when a problem employee really is unmanageable. If the individual is simply arrogant, you can work to help him discover modesty and respect. If it's a case of immaturity, there is plenty of room to help him develop and grow. However, when you find you have exhausted all attempts to give guidance and your development efforts are being rejected, it is time to face the fact that you have on your hands someone who is unmanageable. Recognize it for what it is.

My approach is then relatively straightforward. I quickly initiate the steps for the cure. Make an exit plan and follow it. This means, develop a timetable to have him leave, decide who you will have take over his workload and prepare your team.

When you undertake to move someone like this out of your group, it is essential to be well coordinated with your own manager and your human resources people, because it is important to have strong support. Unmanageables can get the best of you if you slip into considering that their complaints about you may be justified. This self doubt is part of their negative power. A unified message and plan from all parties is the best preparation for a good outcome.

With my plan in place, I then practice my own preaching about giving direct feedback. I make clear to the individual that there is not a bright future for him in the current situation and that change is needed. Change is a challenge for most people and when it is personal it can be extremely difficult. You can expect that denial will be powerful. To manage change in circumstances like this, I recommend clear communication and fast action. Remember that all information leaks and people read non-verbal signals faster then we all think.

In the best of worlds, you will be able to work with the individual in a process of highlighting strengths and finding a position elsewhere that needs those skills. Be prepared that your problem employee may balk at this and make trouble. This is where your colleagues and other managers can help.

Above all, stick with your plan and keep things moving. Be aware that this process typically takes a lot longer than you think it will. Certainly, it will take longer than you want it to.

MY BAD EXPERIENCE

I had an experience with one such unmanageable employee and it had a significant negative impact on my professional and personal life. I let this particular situation get the best of me and for all the wrong reasons.

This person was very demanding and generally negative member of my team who was causing strife in the group. He had experienced early success in another part of the organization and had been moved into my group as a star, which had made him mostly non-responsive to any advice, guidance or management in any form. I found him to have a marked immaturity fatally coupled with a very elevated view of himself.

I tried in many different ways over many months to give him direction but he would have none of it. He made it quite clear to me - and to others - that there was nothing I could teach him.

I saw he was a drag on the team and that our relationship was unsound. I reached the decision that he needed to move to a more promising environment. When I spoke with him to begin the process, his reaction was to turn on me with bitterness and anger. The situation deteriorated into his adopting a toxic mission of wanting to get me out of the way.

My response to being bullied was triggered at this point. This response gets activated for me when I know I am being treated badly or if I feel the need to defend others who are facing something unfair. My anger mounted and I didn't then have the yogic tools to pause, breathe and move forward.

This was all made worse in two ways. First, my own leader was very non-confrontational. In the face of all the vitriol, he pretty much viewed the situation as resulting from my shortcomings and mismanagement. His weakness in standing up to this individual led to my own sense of being ineffective as a leader.

Second, the troublemaker rallied support from senior management. As a previous star performer, he had their ear. He freely conveyed his perception of my incompetence to a senior ally, who then complained on his behalf to my leader's manager.

Many, many difficult months followed, filled with unfair judgments, manipulative behaviors and immaturity on the part of both the unmanageable person and me. Apart from the lack of support from my superiors, the worst for me was seeing the junior employees cringing and wanting to get out of the group. Frankly, it came to a point when I just wanted out as well.

In the end, I gave up. I surrendered. I begged for help from my own manager to get me out of a situation where there was no hope and where I felt I was getting no support.

As it turned out, a truly talented new leader, who recognized that a new place was needed for this unmanageable individual, saved me. Eventually, once my troublemaker accepted that his then-current role was not a good fit for him and that he would go nowhere in my group, he did move on rather quickly.

From what I hear, he is now pretty effective. I count that as a good outcome.

When I think about those difficult times, I am thankful for what I learned from the pain, the tears, the sleepless nights. I know that anger-based responses don't work, are counterproductive and alienate people. Reactions based on anger also degrade a manager's or leader's effectiveness and credibility. Plus, you just feel bad afterwards.

Although I admit I am now actually happy I went through it, I was even happier when the whole episode ended. We all learned from it, hopefully we all grew and the firm was better able to benefit from everyone's talents. The biggest takeaway for me was that when you know that the best thing to do is to change the situation, act quickly. Don't let it drag out. Life is short.

SMARTER THAN YOU

Another version of someone who is unmanageable showed up once when I was managing a global team in London. One of the employees in my group was someone we had recruited from another very different part of the firm. We knew her and we liked her. She was a good salesperson in the sense that she was personable and interacted well with clients.

However, we came to see that she was pretty glib about company products and policies. She happily made promises to clients to do things we could not do and casually misrepresented the capabilities of the firm. We made many efforts to educate her about the limitations she had to observe and to pull her into line. Rarely did she abide by them. The problems multiplied.

At the same time, we learned that this woman spent lots of time conducting personal business while at work. We found she was freely using the company Internet to buy and sell real estate in another European city and to trade in antique furniture. This was blatantly against company policies and we told her to stop. When she didn't, we cut off her Internet access. She then found other ways to do her transactions and did them openly in front of other people in the office.

By now, it was clear we were dealing with someone who was unmanageable. We assessed the problems with her work and the client troubles that had resulted. We coupled that with her insubordination regarding our efforts to curtail her private business activities and we put a termination plan in place.

When we met with her about it, she did the favor of confirming my decision. She announced to me, "You are letting me go because you know I'm a lot smarter than you! And when I get rich and need a large global financial institution, I will not come to you to manage my money!" Of course, that underlined my certainty about moving her out. Life is short.

This particular operator moved on and the last I heard she is now living in Paris selling real estate and antique furniture. I think of it as a great example that there is a place suited for everyone.

Now you have culled the unmanageable ones out of your group and it is problem free. You have been in the fields working closely with your people. You have a good team that's well seasoned and working together smoothly. The time has arrived to help them move onto larger roles.

CHAPTER 9

SERVE THEM UP

CHIANG MAI, THAILAND. I am remembering a biking trip I went on in the mid 1990s on the rural back roads near this town in the golden triangle in northern Thailand. After a morning of cycling, our guide had scheduled a stop for lunch at a place where he knew of a woman who made noodles. We arrived and saw the woman cooking on a hot plate that was set up outdoors on a folding card table. Perhaps our expectations were not high seeing such a primitive kitchen.

What happened next was quite a surprise! With the simplest equipment, this woman made the most amazingly delicious meal I had on my whole visit to Thailand, if not ever. She had total mastery of her cuisine. The noodle dish was simple food, straightforward, perfectly cooked and spiced, not fancy or overly adorned. I will never forget it. One serving cost five cents.

What I love about this memory is that I would never have guessed I would find a meal of that quality in that place and in those conditions. It was a lesson about not discounting a person or a situation based just on the surface impression. The woman was a first-rate chef and a great example that knowing what you're doing leads to excellence.

The meal alone was enough reason to remember this trip but there was more. By some grand coincidence, later that day I received a call at the hotel to be told that I had been promoted to Managing Director. You could call it a good day for me.

SHAKE THINGS UP

I'm thinking about this because now the time has come to evaluate the yield of the nurtured, irrigated seeds and the cultivated and weeded fields. You have your team filled out. In the best of circumstances, each member knows her or his responsibilities and is well trained to execute them. When that is the case, the team hums along without friction and is wonderfully productive.

Take a moment to appreciate that you have planted your garden, tended the crop and seasoned it all to a delectable blend - and that now you can enjoy the fruits of your efforts. But only for a moment!

Exactly at this moment it is time to shake things up. Because you are committed to helping your charges develop and grow, the time has come to serve up the dish. Your management task is to help each one of your people move on to conquer new challenges and keep developing their special skills.

This will keep them from stagnating, getting bored and looking for exits on their own. It is your opportunity to deliver on the trust that has developed between you. Over time, this is good for you too because you attract new top performers to work for you as they see opportunity there.

BREAK IT APART

I consider it a sign of leadership maturity when you are able to focus not just on what you want but also on what is best for your child or student or employee. As the leader, you, yourself, need to be well seasoned enough to accept that as soon as you have everything working well, you have to break it apart.

It is not always the case that managers are committed to making what's good for their people a priority. From time to time over the years, I myself have interviewed for various positions at other firms and, obviously, within my own firm. It is always surprising and disconcerting to me when I meet someone who clearly is most interested in what I can do to make him or her more successful. Such people ask, "What can you do for me?" I am always immediately turned off by this mentality. I have found it interesting to see how pervasive an attitude like this can be. In some organizations it is even the cultural norm.

We all know that timing is everything in serving a well-prepared meal. When the time comes to set the table for your people to start their own next course, you need to let them go and move on to another masterpiece of your own.

HELP THEM FIND A PATHWAY

As I have mentioned, one of my long-standing messages to people I manage is, "The sooner I get rid of you, the happier I will be." I enjoy delivering this message, especially to the very young and ambitious. It always gets quite a reaction. I suppose I should explain that I honestly do mean it. When colleagues outside of my department are sniffing around my people and considering them for other opportunities, I feel I have done my job brilliantly. This is something that has been true for me for years. It not only feeds my firm with the most skilled and well-trained people but it makes my own life much easier because it helps me attract the best talent to my teams. We all win.

How do I encourage the members of my team to find the individual paths that suit them best? By working in the fields I get insight into what each one's path may be. By giving regular feedback and keeping communication access wide open, I can fine tune with each individual.

Recall my advice about "getting over the hump," to just weather the challenge of taking on something new until you find you're in the groove? Training your team members for new roles is an opportunity really to stretch people and that "hump" advice becomes very useful. Remember that smart people grow faster, are happier and succeed more when they move out of their comfort zone. Any new challenge or worthwhile endeavor is generally hard at the beginning and gets worse before it gets better. So while you are managing and training future leaders, remind yourself that they need support and encouragement, especially before you make any judgment about future prospects for anyone. You'll find that there are people who get stuck on their journey over "the hump." Give them time.

When the time is right, I make the effort to help find an opportunity that is best matched for the individual. The more I do this, the easier it is because my colleagues have come to know I have well-groomed candidates who are ready to take on large roles. They regularly turn to me when they need someone to fill a vacated slot or a new position.

BEWARE OF STAGNATION

It's not infrequent that people come back to me for counsel after they've moved on and as a rule I enjoy helping them through their decisions about their next career steps. A bigger problem presents itself when one of my people comes to me after many years of doing the same job to ask for help finding a new position. Usually they have reached a point where they feel that pretty much any different job would be desirable.

When someone has been very specific in his or her role or has been static in the same function for their whole career, it can be a big challenge to give them guidance. It's that much worse when they also have not kept their skills current. To be honest, these types are typically pretty boring people so the challenge can often be more than their skill set!

One good bit of parting advice as you launch your seedlings is to stress the importance of continually expanding their areas of competence to intentionally develop a good mix of skills.

CHAOS

Speaking of "getting over the hump," it is true that sometimes "the hump" may not be a "hump" after all. Sometimes it really is chaos. And sometimes there is pure beauty in total chaos. Periodically, I do need to reflect that the best things about my life were not planned at all.

When people come to me for advice on their careers, it is often at a point when they are deciding among several options. I tell them that I have always believed there is more opportunity in chaos. There is more to learn, more to achieve and more chance to shine. Not all people heed my advice because some prefer to go for things that have more certainty or they want to be part of something that is already a proven success.

Taking the risk of stepping into a situation in disarray requires that you do extra homework before you make the decision. It means you'll have to do research to evaluate the potential reward, including talking with others for advice. You also need to come clean with yourself. Are you willing to take a risk with something new and still messy or are you more comfortable with more certainty and definition? Know which kind of person you are and you'll be equipped to decide about a challenge like this without agonizing over it.

I, myself, have always preferred to take that other road and it has worked well for me. I suppose that is how I became know as "The Fixer." I have always found opportunity in chaos. I also find it is more interesting.

LEADERS ARE MADE, NOT BORN

My definition of a good leader is a person who is talented at motivating a team to produce great work and takes pleasure in their success. This is someone who always makes time for the people he leads, encourages their individual development, is insightful about constructing his crew, is smart about putting individuals together with tasks and generally does all the things I have recommended in the pages of this book!

Some people may not have an interest in such a role. Others may want to be leaders but lack many of the necessary skills. I have stated before that a person has to start with a desire to be a leader in order to do it effectively. I believe that if you are a good leader yourself, you can then identify those with leadership potential.

You should be brutally honest in your assessment of the candidates. I recommend that you give them small tests to see how they deal with disagreement, how they give guidance to others or how they head up a project. Those who have the desire and the talent will quickly come back for more such tests.

A leader is made, not born. It doesn't just happen. It requires work on the part of the future leader and it requires work on your part too. When you spot a good one, you'll do yourself and everyone else a favor when you personally commit to making it happen.

TRAIN YOUR REPLACEMENT

Think how many times you have heard someone say, "No one is irreplaceable." Even when you think it might not be true, it always is. Since everyone is replaceable, you are too. I've seen many examples of this and because there is no way to fight or ignore it, I have always believed it is best to work every day to train that person who might one day replace me.

I think of it in terms of my own self-interest as much as the well being of my group. If you really do want to have the opportunity to advance or explore other opportunities, you need to be conscious of, and perhaps even responsible for, making sure someone else can fill your position.

WHO WILL TAKE YOUR JOB?

Even though I have worked for one firm for more than 32 years, I have had many different roles. The only way I could have moved on from one to the next is that I always had someone ready to take over the spot I was leaving. My company and the industry are filled with people I have managed or mentored. Just recently, when I moved into my latest new role at my company, the person selected to be my successor at my prior position is someone I mentored as a young associate.

I consider it essential, no matter what your job, that you think about what you might do next and who will do what you do now. It may sound very "corporate," but it is important that we all think about succession planning. This clearly is true for large and mid-sized organizations and also for the current and future success of smaller enterprises. Even if you are an independent one-woman veterinary office, it is probably a good idea to have a back-up relationship with another local vet just in case of illness or emergencies. It is always wise for small organizations and one-person shops to foster relationships with others in their same or similar endeavors.

My commitment to help everyone grow means I believe someone in my group should be able to take over my own job. Such a belief will strengthen the bonds you have with those you lead, as they can feel your willingness to further their careers by expanding their responsibilities and knowledge. Frankly, it also makes your life a whole lot easier, as you can delegate more and more.

To say you should be training your replacement every day may sound like the voice of an old secure person speaking from on high. I understand that this may sound suicidal to some people but I believe that it is the right thing to do. I am not sure where I got such confidence. I know that I like change and I view someone seeking to take my job as the insurance I need to keep change coming.

I WILL WORK FOR YOU ONE DAY

"If I do my job well, I will work for you one day." This is another of my messages about moving people on to bigger and better things. I don't necessarily mean this literally but more as an aspiration that I have for everybody.

The reaction I get to this tells me a lot about who somebody is and what I can expect from him or her. I find that confident people get it but as a rule insecure people don't. I remember delivering this message to a young "superstar" who I had just started managing. I knew we were headed for a challenging relationship the minute I said it from his cocky chuckle of disbelief.

The reality is that some people – your employees, your colleagues or your own manager – may struggle to accept the fact that you are secure enough in your own skin to aspire some day to work for someone who currently works for you. I do believe that this is largely a maturity issue and, in truth, perhaps I wasn't so secure when I was 20 years younger.

KNOWING WHEN TO LEAVE

Being ready yourself to make the decision to move on ensures that you can relate to your people's mindsets as they consider their career moves. I have moved to new roles regularly during my career and am doing so again with my recent decision to leave my long-term employer.

I thought about this when Pope Benedict XVI stunned the world by announcing his resignation. In fact, I was surprised how much I related to his decision. Both of us chose to give up our day jobs and enter into our transitions. I am somewhat younger than the Pope, so there was no health reason that factored into my conclusion to give up my long-time career. Could it be that this was the only serious difference?

Both of us no longer have to sit through long meetings packed with too many people. Perhaps he got impatient with big bureaucracy and multiple decision makers?

When making planned life changes, it is good if you are motivated by a desire to move toward endeavors that are new and exciting. It is best not to do it because you are running away from something. It's even worse to give up what you love because you have lost your tolerance for suffering the fools around you.

I debated these issues with myself when I decided to make my recent changes. I recognized that I had lost patience with what I was doing. Being patient is essential to letting organizations or people ripen. Some things you just can't hurry along; they need their own good time. I knew that I had to get patience back into my life. I was fortunate to have started many new and exciting projects, so my focus was already on the bright future before me.

Both the Pope and I had a desire to leave quietly. I wanted no celebrations of my retirement and happily it worked out that way. The Pope chose to leave public life completely. As I write, I am up in the woods with my favorite, four-legged companions in contemplation of this issue and others. We know the Pope will spend hours also in quiet contemplation as he prays and meditates. Perhaps I should suggest some gentle Yoga as well? I wonder if the Pope has a dog.

As I move onto my own new path and look back, there is no question that my proudest achievement has been mentoring the tremendous talent I encountered over my 32 years. My hope is that all those talented younger colleagues get the opportunity to have their time to shine and to give similar opportunities to others.

The recipe is complete and now it's up to you to change around its ingredients in order to make your own plate of perfect noodles. To help you with that, I'll move on to my identification of the six Types of people you're likely to encounter in the workplace.

THE TYPES

CHAPTER 1 0

JUST MY TYPE!

PARIS, FRANCE. I'm in Paris on vacation with some good friends. It's been 10 years since I was last here. Walking around this beautiful city, I'm struck with the huge variety of people I'm seeing.

It turns out that Paris is the most visited city in the world, so that makes sense to me as I tour the historical sites, museums and shopping venues where most of the people we encounter are foreign tourists. It makes even more sense when I find out that this is one of the most multi-cultural cities in Europe with an immigrant population of about 20 percent. They are Algerian, Vietnamese, Chinese, Portuguese, Northern and Western African and increasingly Latin American.

Of course, living in New York City I am used to being surrounded by people of all different kinds. Even growing up in Philadelphia, I was accustomed to crowds of people visiting the tourist attractions. What is new to me is the diversity of the people who call Paris home. I guess I'm surprised because I have a well-etched idea of a Parisian. It's a bit of a stereotype with elements of French pride and sophistication and appreciation of fine food and wine.

Such stereotypes can get in the way of being open to people of different backgrounds. Yet sometimes they can be useful as a shorthand way to help you get your bearings in an unfamiliar environment. What I know is that this technique applies to more than nationalities.

PATTERNS

You know how sometimes a person you've just met reminds you of someone else you already know? Not how he looks but how he acts? One fellow may be very outgoing, noisy and friendly to everyone while another may be quiet and self-contained. This one may be a meticulous rule-follower while the next one takes shortcuts and a third one is creative in untraditional ways. Someone intimidates those around her and someone else keeps goofing off.

Parents, teachers, coaches, managers and leaders see these differences regularly. We all start learning about this when we are kids interacting with our siblings, cousins, playmates, classmates and teammates. We continue to experience it with the members of the groups we join and the organizations we participate in at all stages of our lives. It is no different in the workplace.

Over my many working years, I have noticed distinct characteristics and behaviors in the people I've encountered. I have spotted them again and then again. I have gradually come to realize that these characteristics and behaviors fall into patterns. These patterns show up in colleagues, the people I report to, my vendors, clients and other business associates. They are very clear in the people I manage. I learned it is possible to anticipate how people who exhibit a certain pattern will act in various circumstances and to understand what I might expect from them.

I have used these patterns as a basis for identifying specific Types of people. Through the years I have learned to spot them quickly when I meet someone new. I have found that the more skilled you become at spotting what Type a person is, the more likely you will have success managing her. Starting right from the interview, you can adjust your approach for the particular kind of individual you are assessing. This will make you better able to flush out her strengths and her shortcomings. As a result, you will have more insight about what to expect from her.

SHAPING YOUR APPROACH

Just as I came to recognize the Types, I also learned how to be most effective in working with each of them. I have learned that they need to be handled differently from each other. While one management tactic may work brilliantly with one Type, it can prove utterly useless with another.

The fancy princess who expects all things delivered on a golden platter will have to be reined in and you will need to work constantly to temper her outsized expectations. The skinny guy who speaks softly and keeps saying "Sorry" will need to be drawn out and given extra encouragement. There will be times when you will have to exert firm resistance to put the brakes on the woman with her chin and elbows sticking out along with her harmful attitudes. There will be other times when you will have to point out repeated lack of results to the cheery fellow who jabbers on about all his big ideas, to let him know you are not being fooled.

As a leader, you have to balance all this with delivering rewards duly earned and fostering each individual to develop new skills and grow. To effectively build and shape your gang, you need to consider how one Type interacts with another. This will make you more effective in managing them and help you head off dysfunctional groupings.

DON'T RUSH TO JUDGMENT

I have a word of caution about identifying Types. Managers, colleagues, coaches, mentors, teachers and all leaders all need to give everyone a fair chance to show who they are and what they can do. It's essential to keep your mind open as you get to know the individuals you lead and not jump to conclusions about their potential based solely on what Type they are.

There are certain jobs that require quick judgment. If you are an emergency room doctor, an air traffic controller or a stock trader on a financial exchange, your ability to make quick decisions is an integral part of what you do. Your success should not be based on one or two smart or faulty tactical choices but rather on your history of consistently prudent decisions.

What concerns me is when a colleague or manager makes a few short-term observations of an individual's performance and then uses those as the basis of his long-term opinion of that person. This may be a positive or negative opinion. Either way, it is disheartening when you hear people discount or overrate someone's potential based on just one or two examples of his or her work.

It is even more frustrating when you find that those who make these snap judgments seem incapable of ever changing their minds. When you are a manager of someone whom you feel has been unfairly judged and you have aspirations for him, this can be very painful. Conversely, it can be frustrating to see someone benefit too much from just a few positive observations, though those individuals typically get right-sized once they don't deliver.

I am not advocating that you simply slap a "Type" label onto people and then treat them with cookie-cutter sameness. You know my very strong advocacy of working in the fields to get to know each member of your group individually, understand the details of the work each one does and the way she or he does it. At the same time, I believe that recognizing the Type each person resembles will help you modify your style for managing that person effectively.

WHAT TYPE ARE YOU?

While they can be divided and subdivided into many groups, I have distinguished six distinct Types that I have come across most frequently and that have been the most challenging for me to manage.

I have given the six Types names that help as a shorthand to identify their behaviors. I call them:

- The Outperformer
- The Underperformer
- The Entitled
- The Fluffer
- The Bully
- The Lone Ranger

In the next six chapters, you will see the Types described and characterized. They are illustrated with anecdotes from my working life and from the experiences of those in other lines of work whom I have interviewed for this book. I describe the approaches I have developed for managing them, specifically geared for the particular attributes of each Type, and I give guidance about each Type as a leader.

Becoming aware of what Types your students, team members, friends, employees and colleagues are will give you helpful insights into their behaviors. This will make you better equipped to select management techniques that are suited to their needs and to provide the thoughtful guidance that will lead them to success.

CHAPTER 11

THE OUTPERFORMER - DON'T NEGLECT

BANGALORE, INDIA. I am spending a few weeks at an ashram in India. I have come to Bangalore to deepen my yoga practice, learn more about meditation and to spend some focused time writing this book. This ashram hotel is wonderfully run. Even though there are only a half dozen guests here right now, the staff members are providing services as if the hotel were full.

When people hear that I practice yoga, I often get comments like, "I am not flexible so I couldn't so that." Or, "I would be too embarrassed to try because I would not be good enough." This sort of reasoning is off the mark, because yoga is not meant to be a competition. It is something that you learn and then you get more seasoned and perhaps even proficient. But it is always considered a "practice."

COMPETITIVE ENERGIES

Yoga may be one of the few endeavors in life that is not a competition. We all know that we start being competitive from a very young age. Some people become more and more so as they get older. If those competitive energies are well directed, they can contribute to great success. Competitive students, employees and leaders are those who are most likely to outperform their peers.

Now of course you are eager to read about the Type that I call the Outperformer because you consider it to be about the Type that most describes you! Just like the staff at the Ashram here, you are all Outperformers. Of course you are! Surely your parents and teachers told you this?

FIRST GRADE

There have been times in my life when I have been an Outperformer (just as there have been times when I have been an Underperformer.) My earliest recollection of being an Outperformer was when I was just finishing first grade. I didn't go to kindergarten so first grade was literally my first year of formal classroom learning. That whole year, I just went about my business and did whatever I was asked in a class of 71 children. This was the tail end of the baby boom and in my school in Philadelphia there were six first grade classes, each with 60 to 75 students.

At the end of the year, the whole school assembled in the gymnasium (or maybe it was in the church, given this was a Catholic school). I was taken aside and told to take a special seat at the front. I didn't know why I was being separated from the others in my class. I had no idea that I was about to get an award for having the "highest general average" of the first grade. I remember this as the first time I ever thought I might have some special ability. I was a six-year-old Outperformer!

SIXTH GRADE

This academic excellence continued without effort until the sixth grade. That year, I was amazed to find out I had just barely made it into the top-tier class, as I had done for all of the previous five years. It was then, at age 11, when I first came to the realization that you really need to make an effort in order to excel. So I did and I guess I never stopped.

In my case, it was my own surprise at nearly falling short that was the kick in the pants. Parents, teachers and managers can help the child, student or employee develop self-awareness about the relationship of effort to outcomes and give encouragement to keep it up.

THE BEST

You are reading this book because you know that you are great and that you just need a few tips to sharpen your management skills, right? But wait! Everyone can't be The Best. Many people are average and that is perfectly acceptable. At the end of this book, you will read how there is a place for everyone, provided they are managed in a way that sets them up to succeed.

Lots of people firmly believe they are The Best and don't want to be told otherwise. Many of them do indeed merit the designation Outperformer. You have surely encountered this Type in school or on a sports team or in another group you belonged to as a child. You may even have had the excruciating experience of having a sibling like this in your family! This was the pain-in-the-ass kid who always did everything perfectly. She had her homework done on time and she knew all the answers in class. He won the races and scored the most points and was smart about strategy in the sports event. She memorized all the notes in the orchestra piece and played them flawlessly. He was elected president of the club.

It is not unusual for people with competitive personalities to experience the intense pressures that come with a focus on winning or getting the best grades. Learning to handle such pressures becomes one of their strengths. This Type usually gets lots of attention and praise from parents, coaches and teachers. Later, this Type can show up in the workplace as an Outperformer.

CHARACTERISTICS

There are plenty of characteristics I could use to describe this Type, but let's look at three key ones. Outperformers tend to:

- Get good grades their whole life and become accustomed to being told they are wonderful.
- Be highly competitive.
- Become "addicted" to being The Best and always rewarded.

There are some ways to spot an Outperformer in the interview process. Of course you'll have an early warning when someone comes recommended as a star. Your Outperformer antennae should be on alert if you notice that the candidate is super quick to grasp the details of the job based just on meeting with your interview team. This suggests a powerful ability to listen as well as to think quickly. Another good sign is if the individual is able to make independent suggestions during your interview meetings.

You might think these are easy people to manage. This can be true but it is not necessarily so. Outperformers present some special challenges. That competitive characteristic can make them difficult to manage.

OUTPERFORMER NEGLECT

Parents, teachers, managers and leaders are generally good at recognizing star performers in the short term. Where it can get tricky – and where I think leaders fall short with those individuals who always get A's or consistently beat all sales targets or build the best products and generally excel in whatever they do – is in actively managing them over long periods of time. Significant management mis-steps come from what I call Outperformer Neglect. Unfortunately, this error is committed all too often.

PAY ATTENTION

Many parents and leaders are conscientious about giving attention to those who obviously need it. Those are the students who need help just to get a passing grade or employees who need more training just to perform in their job at a satisfactory level. The danger is that this kind of management focus can happen at the expense of keeping current with your best people.

It's a big risk to assume that all overachievers really know they are doing well and that they have sufficient motivation to continue doing so. Even the stars need praise. You need to remember to tell them explicitly that they are doing a great job. This assurance will give them confidence that what they are doing is on the mark and will comfort them that you recognize their excellence. Even though it is obvious to you that they are outstanding, they won't know that you see it unless you tell them.

Don't just assume they know. Remember, they're used to being told they are wonderful.

PRAISE

This praise needs to be given enthusiastically and more frequently than you might think. You need to check the temperature of the Outperformer often. Otherwise, these folks can get lazy or, in the case of a child or student, they can act out in ways you might find surprising and perhaps destructive

I always make it a point to call an Outperformer aside and then mention her wonderfulness. I ask my assistant to request that she come into my office and of course she shows up with a notebook, ready for me to dispense some wisdom or a task. I then just look at her and say, "You know, Trixie, you are doing a phenomenal job. Just thought I would tell you that." It is always very much appreciated.

Most of my managers rarely told me much about how I was doing. I once had a manager who told me he was surprised that, after so many years in the business, I still needed to be reminded that I was doing great. I did need to be told. It always feels really good to hear it.

SET THE TEMPO

An Outperformer with a very promising future can be impatient. You as the manager or teacher of such a star need to set the pace for moving forward. Perhaps you yourself are so excited about her that you give her too much responsibility or independence too soon. If she is a super producer, you may feel it is a natural progression to give her a few people to manage. If someone has completed a mega-project with great success, you may agree to let him take on more responsibility. But perhaps they were not ready.

You need to think about this when challenging your stars. Many times, these situations can go wrong because you assume too much or you forget to be diligent about managing the transitions for these individuals. Managers too often extrapolate one kind of success by an Outperformer and assume a similar level of success can be achieved when they do something else, no matter what you throw at them. This is another kind of Outperformer Neglect and it happens too often.

Those best people need to know what the future should hold for them and this includes managing the time frame for their next milestone or advancement. If you don't set the tempo for them, you can risk seeing their performance degrade, perhaps to test your judgment or maybe just to get attention. This may be true for a child, student, soldier, businessperson, anyone.

MANAGE EXPECTATIONS

You need to manage the expectations of the consistently strong players thoughtfully and frequently. In the workplace, if you don't do this properly, you also risk losing them to other employers. Your Outperformers need to be handled so they can be realistic about when they might achieve bigger things - more responsibilities, higher compensation or any other goals. They probably actually need more specifics, more frequently, than your Underperformers. Otherwise, they may express their disappointment by leaving even when you might be thinking they are the happiest people you have.

The grass may appear greener elsewhere to a star if no one reminds her that she is already firmly planted in a pretty green place. Don't take your Outperformers for granted and always provide them opportunities to stretch.

INHERITING THE MESS

My most challenging Outperformer situations have come when another manager has made assumptions about a star, has pushed her too fast and then has turned her over to me to manage. This problem can be really tough because she may arrive discouraged or angry or confused and require lots of attention and conversations and interventions.

Sometimes an individual in this situation becomes unmanageable, as I have discussed in the chapter called Weed Them Out. Many times people who get caught up in this kind of mess are true stars but got misdirected to roles for which they may not have been suited.

"BIG DISEASE"

A common experience I have had with the Outperformer Type is when someone gets what I call "big disease." The individual has all the right skills, is performing on all fronts and is evolving nicely into his new responsibilities. He is just still immature for the "big" role.

When I stretch someone this way, I have to remind myself that I have put him in a role that may be beyond him and he may react by doing unexpected things. This can take the form of his micromanaging others, becoming stubborn, thinking he has nothing to learn, failing to keep his manager informed, becoming grandiose, taking imprudent risks or making decisions without bringing others into the discussions.

This kind of situation can develop as the result of neglect by his manager. It is important to be very conscious of preventing this because you don't want to have to get involved in major damage control that could slow down what was a career with great momentum.

THIS IS EASY

I know of a superstar Outperformer whose career I monitor closely. When he was a smarty-pants analyst just out of college, he was able to quickly perform all kinds of sophisticated analyses of issues and take on responsibilities far faster than anyone I had seen before. However, he hadn't yet learned that in order to be successful in the long term he needed to know details and he needed to know how to express them. This kid had a cocky, "this is easy" attitude going on. He was the junior person on the team, yet that did not prevent me from aggressively stretching him. At the same time, I did not exempt him from the need to make presentation slides and enhance his communication skills.

One day, I gave him some feedback about this right after a meeting ended. He very strongly took issue with my criticism of both the quality of a presentation he had just delivered and the way he had explained it to the team.

He said, "Well I am not really into that slide making thing."

My response was, "Well, you need to get into it right away."

I suggested that he take a course or perhaps teach himself starting that day. We then began a schedule of regular reviews of his slides and rehearsals of his presentations. He did become reasonably proficient at making presentation slides and I know he became incredibly effective in delivering what are often complicated messages. In this example, we slowed the tempo of his advancement, enhanced a few skills and moved forward. His star continues to rise.

BEWARE OF DENIAL

Competitive people are generally happy when they are doing something they are very talented at. When they come up against something they need to improve on or something they haven't mastered yet, things can get tough. I have found that Outperformers often struggle to take constructive feedback. They are likely to hear it only as negative.

This is especially striking to me as I do my yoga here in India because it is in stark contrast to the yoga mindset, which teaches that improvement is always possible and is to be continuously pursued. A constructive suggestion is a welcome gift to a yogi.

GIVE IT TO THEM

The single most important thing about performance feedback to this Type (or to any Type for that matter) is to *do it now*! I can't stress this enough. As I have said, feedback needs to be given continuously and in the moment, not deferred for a special performance review. I find that immediate, constructive, balanced feedback is the best way to address undesirable performance and is also super effective for reinforcing the positive.

Particularly with the Outperformer, managers can be reluctant to do this. They may shy away from a long discussion or even an argument with a star. But they are doing no favor to anyone this way. Performance "metrics" and feedback are key to letting your people develop and grow. In their absence, even your stars often will feel clueless as to whether or not they are doing the right things.

DEEP DENIAL

Of course, there are people who do get the regular feedback, but are in denial about the issues they need to address. Some of the most challenging and lengthy conversations I have had with star employees over my three decades have been those involving simple suggestions of "constructive improvements."

Denial can be a pretty well developed muscle with this Type. Some can't take criticism at all. I have given a message as simple as, "You are amazingly, wonderfully super, but you are not The Best." An hour later I was still in a conference room discussing the whole issue.

This is especially true for junior people who are early in their careers. Generally, people of this Type were rarely if ever told that they were anything less than perfect. I had a young analyst many years ago who practically bit my head off after she read her first ever performance review. It wasn't like there was anything serious in it that would indicate failure. Instead, it pointed out various things that she should strive to do better and some teamwork issues she needed to address. All of it was quite typical for someone at that stage of her career.

For weeks and months, I had to hear about this review! She is currently a super successful leader in her industry. To this day, about 20 years later, I still have to hear about that review, although we do laugh about it now. Perhaps I should read it again to see if she ever did go on to address all of the issues I outlined.

LET IT SIT

When you encounter this problem of denial with an Outperformer - and you will - the best response is to let things sit. Give the feedback and then move away from it. Later, come back and continue the conversation, repeatedly if necessary. Many times you will see the denial diminish incrementally or even change completely. For some people, there may not be any change, which will have longer-term ramifications for that person's future. In this case, you will need to reassess their role.

I would say that the best Outperformer is one who has a ton of positive qualities and also, especially, the ability to recognize, accept and work on the things they could improve.

ARE THEY ORGANIZED?

Assessing someone's organization skills is simple and important. Perhaps it is a good first metric for the consideration of whether your star performer has the makeup to become a leader. I have learned that to be really effective as a manager on a sustainable basis, you need to be organized.

I have had many managers in my career and I have had the benefit of working with excellent leaders and some really poor ones. The great ones were all extremely well organized, the poor ones not so. My experiences with leaders who lacked a good sense of organization always felt like we spent lots of time talking a good game but we never really seemed to know where we were going and we usually didn't get very far.

I am sure there were times that I was an underachiever but one thing I am confident about is that I am very organized. I may even be too organized, to the point where I struggle to sit still and relax. This is clearly why I find yoga and meditation so beneficial. I have been like this my whole life. It showed when I took multiple inventories of my Halloween candy when I was young. It was behind my mailing a thousand resumes to find a job as I was graduating from college. I depended on these abilities to be able to work at a full time job while I was going to college.

In my professional life, I maintain "to do" lists, I meet all deadlines, I have daily routines for gathering information and I use various systems to keep things orderly. Some telltale signs of someone who is not organized are: they have a messy desk or work space; they are always rushing, getting things ready at the last minute or missing deadlines; they are sloppy with details; or they show a lack of thoughtful prioritization of tasks or projects.

Being organized comes naturally to some and may be a struggle for others. I believe that good organizational skills can be learned and that with the right tools and a commitment to get and stay organized, anyone can do it. If you have an Outperformer with great potential who is lacking in this area but who has the desire and the other skills to be a leader, get him some help learning to be organized. It is worth the effort.

THE OUTPERFORMER AS LEADER

It's logical to think that this Type will make a good leader. Sometimes they do. Their qualities of being smart, insightful, quick and committed to success can be a winning combination in managing a group.

However, it is a common mistake that we make all too often to assume that all Outperformers can be great managers. The truth is, stars may not necessarily make good leaders. Remember the saying, "The best salesman does not necessarily make a good sales manager."

As I was making that list of Outperformer characteristics at the beginning of this chapter, I thought of lots more things that could be on it.

- They aren't all necessarily articulate or good public speakers.
- They aren't all good team players.
- They don't always naturally help others or even want to see others succeed.

These are problems that can get in the way of their becoming good leaders. So can the high standards the Outperformer assumes, based on her history of excelling at whatever she takes on. In a team, there will be varied abilities and a star's frustration that everyone doesn't measure up to her own expectations can be a problem.

ON HER OWN

Sometimes an Outperformer feels she is so good at what she does that she heads out on her own, shunning the rest of the team. This is an Outperformer version of the Type that I call The Lone Ranger. When someone does this, the team as a whole suffers. For sure, this is not someone who should be put in a leadership position. Someone like this can even turn out to be unmanageable. For the manager, this is an opportunity to teach the star the importance of teamwork.

If you have an Outperformer who really doesn't want to be a manager or lacks the skills, it is your responsibility carefully and creatively to set her expectations for continued success in other ways in the future. There is a place for her too.

SOMETIMES A STAR IS JUST A STAR

In order for high achievers to also be great managers, they have to really care not only about their own success but also get happiness from the successes of others. This leads to the high achiever working with the team to bring about even greater achievements. When this happens, you may have a great leader in the making.

An Outperformer who possesses these qualities can go on to be an outstanding manager. It is a special person who can pull this off. I suppose this is why, when I am a fan of a leader, I tend to be a really big fan.

THE OUTPERFORMER
ADVICE SUMMARY

My best advice about how to manage the Type that is the Outperformer is to:

- Avoid committing Outperformer Neglect. Even the stars need praise.
- Check in often. Manage expectations.
- Give frequent, immediate, direct feedback. Even though they are high performing, they still need to know how they are doing.
- Beware of denial. Make sure they know what needs work.
- Set the tempo. Resist promotion too early.
- Be alert to "big disease."
- Encourage them to be organized.
- Make a distinction between stars and leaders.

CHAPTER 12

THE UNDERPERFORMER – MAKE HIM SPEAK

NOSARA, COSTA RICA. It's frustrating when you go on a vacation and it turns out to be a disappointment. This rarely happens to me any more because I tend to go on yoga-related vacations and most yogis tend to be reasonably accepting of setbacks and inconvenience. But this time it was just too much even for me.

I came to Costa Rica to a yoga retreat. As it turned out, there were two primary challenges. First, although the facility was relatively new, some of it was very badly designed. Some rooms, including mine, had no air conditioning and were also poorly ventilated, making it impossible to sleep in the very uncomfortable heat. The place looked beautiful but with lack of rest, who could appreciate that?

The second reason for disappointment came from the instructors. I knew both of them and I had been on yoga trips with each of them previously but at separate times. On this trip, as a teaching team guiding a very large group, they lacked cohesiveness and consistency. It was distracting. They were ineffective.

Between the heat, lack of sleep and lack of inspiration from the teachers, I decided it was just too much, so I left the place a few days early. This is very unlike me because I can usually make the best of any situation. I booked myself a room at a hotel on another part of the island in hopes of having some rest and peaceful yoga before the week's end.

The trip to the hotel took several hours and during it I started thinking about why the yoga teachers had "underperformed." Had they not prepared? Did they just think that two instructors were better than one? Was there something about the composition or size of the group that they did not assess adequately? More importantly, I wonder if they even knew that some people were leaving because of disappointment.

DISAPPOINTMENT

Welcome to one of my flaws. My challenge with disappointment is not so much related to my own performance as it is with being disappointed in someone I manage. Such disappointment comes when an employee, colleague, student or child performs at a level that is less than you believe or know she can achieve. This is like the feeling a parent gets when their kid brings home a poor report card. I get a mildly sick feeling in my stomach and then promptly begin the mental gymnastics of assembling constructive things I will say to the individual to help him "want" to do better.

This experience of disappointment may be true for parents, teachers or anyone charged with leading others. It also extends to managing any relationship you might have with any person or pet and is even relevant for managing yourself. I have to admit to an example in my own behavior. I find it enormously ironic that I have underperformed by letting much time go by before completing the writing of this chapter! My disappointment in having such a struggle with the actual writing has not matched my much greater disappointment that I was unable to get it done in the amount of time I expected. Then I forgave myself, got to work and finished it up.

CHALLENGE

You've seen the Type that I call the Underperformer in school or on the team or in other groups. Sometimes you've thought of him as lazy or not so smart. He's the one who didn't do the homework or "forgot" to bring it to class. She can't remember her lines in the drama club play. Maybe he misses practice for the big game or gets mad at the coach because he really doesn't want to play baseball. Often, it seems like she's just not paying attention.

Underperformers can be a serious challenge for parents, teachers, coaches, managers and other leaders. Often, they are highly capable but just don't deliver. Coming to terms with your own disappointment as a leader is prerequisite to helping the individual. You must be sure you are clear of your own need to have him do well and separate that from the actual facts of his performance. This comes with maturity as a manager or teacher. Understanding the reason someone falls into this Type, as I set forth below, will help.

CHARACTERISTICS

The manager, teacher or leader of an Underperformer can recognize as characteristics that they tend to:

- Perform their work poorly.
- Fail to progress as expected.
- Have a lackluster attitude.
- Be frequently distracted.
- Be reluctant to talk about their performance.

It can be very hard to predict during the interview process that someone will turn out to be an Underperformer. One telltale sign may be that he diverts the interview to something he wants to talk about instead of answering your questions. Another is when he uses lingo related to his current job or employer without broadening his thinking to the actual conversation he's having with you. You may be tipped off if he doesn't seem to grasp the responsibilities of the job that's been described to him during the interviews. If these signs show up, it's an instance where getting several references is especially important. If you still have doubts, you may want to ask him to speak in front of a group or do an appropriate test of some kind.

SELF-AWARENESS

One of the characteristics of an Underperformer can be the inability, or refusal, to take an honest look at himself. If he doesn't look, he has little chance of realizing he has shortcomings.

LOOKIN' GLASS

This brings me to a story about my Grandma Ruth, who always seemed to flip us some form of wisdom when we least expected it. One day my sister was visiting her and noticed a large mirror that was leaning against a wall in her living room, on the floor behind a sofa. It was of no use behind that old sofa, so my sister asked if she could have it for her house. In response, Grandma Ruth said, "Kaaathi, what'ya want with that ole lookin' glaaas? Ya gonna look at yourself?"

The Underperformer needs to be aware of problematic things he is doing, such as missing deadlines, having misunderstandings, making errors or showing an inability to get along with his colleagues. Without that self-reflection, he has little chance of making an improvement.

How many of us are able to take an honest look at our self and our performance as a student or manager or friend or partner? Do you honestly know your best attributes, talents and abilities? Are you aware of your flaws and limitations?

MAKE HIM SPEAK!

It is not uncommon that, even if he does know some of his shortcomings, an Underperformer will be very reluctant to talk about them. When you suspect you are managing an Underperformer, you should immediately spend time with him to discuss it. Make him speak!

Sometimes it can be tricky to distinguish an Underperformer from someone who is just shy. You never know what brilliance lies within someone who doesn't always speak up. Drawing him out is the way to help him become aware of a problem and the opportunities for correcting it. He may have spent considerable effort focused on important work – and done it well. Make him speak! Everyone deserves the opportunity to shine and sufficient face time to present the result of his efforts.

Conversely, you want to avoid being disappointed by the real Underperformer who didn't do enough focused preparation or planning. You certainly don't want to be surprised by a shortage of details or be on the hook when the inflated sales targets are not met. Make him speak!

THE BENT GIRAFFE

Self-awareness extends to matters of personal interactions as well. I remember many years ago I had a colleague who lacked a sense of the appropriate level of "social space" between herself and someone she might be speaking with. Her face would draw uncomfortably close during a conversation. At one work function, a group of us spent the evening watching this individual getting "close" to people. We saw her victims squirm to position themselves at a "normal" distance. I remember one guy getting trapped against a wall. In one conversation, the "in your face" woman actually leaned forward to get her point more directly in line with the face of the shorter man she was addressing. She looked like a bent giraffe! Of course, the problem was that people were uncomfortable and didn't want to interact with her. This left her ineffective in accomplishing her work.

Being self-aware means having a clear understanding of your strengths and weaknesses. Then, you have a chance to figure out what you need to work on and you can seek help in doing it.

NOT ME!

Many people, even those who are self-aware, may not know they are not performing as expected. Most people don't think of themselves as belonging to this Type. The starting point for working with them to do better is to be sure they know that they are not up to snuff. How does someone know that she is not performing up to expectations?

As you know, I set a high value on the importance of frequent feedback. If you are giving feedback regularly to your underperforming children, students or employees, they should know when they are not performing well. One of the prerequisites to helping an Underperformer improve is to be sure she understands exactly how she is doing. Delivering the message is the first step. Of course this is not necessarily easy. The manager's skills at giving direct, constructive, balanced feedback come into full play with Underperformers. How that information is communicated and received is fundamental to moving forward.

In the case of disappointing news, it is best to deliver it directly. Don't avoid the conversation. Think of it as a way to strengthen the connection you have with the child, student or employee. Delivering disappointing news with thoughtful planning can actually strengthen the relationship. It can build mutual respect and trust. It will show that you are interested in her future and give her hope.

As a manager or leader of this Type, I find it is best to be very honest and open with your feedback, especially if someone explicitly asks for it. The worst you can do is to ignore an Underperformer or put off the difficult conversations. Avoidance, sugar coating or delay just make it harder for you to convey the necessary message and more difficult for the Underperformer to accept it. This is detrimental to the individual and to the dynamics of the team all around.

WHAT TO DO

So you give the feedback. The question then becomes, what does the individual do with that information? Is it accepted or denied? Does the person getting the message welcome suggestions about how to get better? Or does he want to spend time refuting the feedback?

DENIAL AND HIDING

Denial can be a factor with the Underperformer just as with every other Type and this can lead him to be disruptive, especially if he won't speak up about it. The most important thing you need to do as a manager is to consistently deliver the unvarnished review and then get the individual to talk about the issue.

On the other hand, sometimes the Underperformer knows he is bad at what he does. He may adopt a Lone Ranger tactic of snubbing the team to hide the fact. He goes off on his own, shielding his substandard work from the view of the others. A sharp-eyed manager will notice this and may also be alerted to the behavior by other members of the team.

PASSIVE AND AGGRESSIVE

If you have an Underperformer who is also passive, you will find it pretty difficult to help him. Typically, it's not just that he doesn't realize he is not doing well or that he is in denial about it. Worse, it's that he says very little when you discuss it with him. Without his response to your feedback, you have nothing substantial to work with. You need him to engage with the issue. Make him speak! If he just won't, there's little you can do. It's sort of like trying to repair a car with no tools.

An aggressive Underperformer, on the other hand, is fun to work with because she will typically deny, protest, point blame and rationalize. This gives you, as the parent, teacher or leader, lots of material, provided by her, that you can use to address her issues.

An Underperformer who is also passive-aggressive is the toughest. You have to be really careful with this creatively crafty laggard. This kind of Underperformer may very well turn out to be unmanageable and be the one you want to manage out of your group.

TURN IT AROUND

To think about how to turn an Underperformer into a productive team member, I find it is essential first to come to terms with the reason someone may fall into this Type. Although there can be many, many reasons, I have found I can group them into three overall categories: outside issues, boredom and mismatch.

The measures that will prove most useful to help this Type vary with the reason they are underperforming. Your job is to be wise in selecting the appropriate ones. However, as you can guess and as you will see, feedback is central to all of them.

OUTSIDE ISSUES

It is, of course, well known that things going on in a person's life outside of the schoolroom or workplace can have a big influence on that individual's performance. It seems hard to believe we don't recognize that things like conflict in our personal life, worries about health matters, concern about finances and many other issues can distract us from our focus on the job. It seems so obvious but the reality is that we very often forget. We not only forget as it applies to ourselves but we forget how important it is to those we parent, teach and lead.

LACK OF SLEEP

I have found that the most common outside issue is a lack of sleep. This can result from any number of things. For me at the yoga retreat, it was physical discomfort because of the heat. Lots of times unresolved personal issues can disrupt a person's sleep. Life events like a new baby, a difficult personal relationship, a family illness or moving to a new place to live can do it too.

Whatever the reason, lack of rest pretty predictably results in diminished focus. We're just not as sharp, don't think as clearly and don't reason as well when we're overtired. How can we make rational decisions with no sleep?

NOT A PRETTY PICTURE

Of course there are many outside issues other than lack of sleep that can have the same result. When I left the "underperforming" yoga retreat and moved to this upscale resort to get some rest, I was struck by the abundance of golf courses surrounding the hotel. The golf courses reminded me of Tiger Woods and he provides me with a persuasive example of the impact of outside issues and the resulting lack of focus on performance. In the case of golf, the score tells the story.

Outside issues can make someone an Underperformer intermittently or for only a particular period. I know that I personally have been an Underperformer several times during my long career. I am not afraid to admit it and I am pretty confident I could tell you the details of each time it happened. In some cases I had an underperforming boss, in others I was just bored. Most of the time it was when there was external "stuff' going on in my life that was very distracting and resulted in a lack of rest.

As a rule, I am one of those people who can perform at a high level with very little sleep but when the lack of rest is paired with the distraction of outside issues, the result is a loss of focus and it is not a pretty picture. What happens is that I get impatient with the indecisiveness of groupthink; my rabid desire to get results quickly gets more intense; and worse, I write long emails on topics that are best discussed in person.

ACT NOW

If something does come up in a person's outside life that distracts him from his job, the sooner you know about it, the better for him and the team. This is a case where staying close to your people in the fields pays off. It may be appropriate to recommend, or even insist, that he take some vacation time to resolve the issue and, importantly, catch up on sleep. When he comes back refreshed, you can assess if that was the actual reason for the poor performance.

I have gathered lots of examples of Underperformers who are shocked when they are told so. They just don't get how they can give their every waking moment to a career or job and then be told they are actually not doing so well. Many times they felt like they deserved a pass because of their time commitment. Of course, putting in the time, or working hard, is not the same as performing well.

WORK-LIFE JUGGLING

"All work and no play makes Jack a dull boy!" As a responsible parent, manager or leader of any kind, you must see to it that your charges don't "overdo it." Spending too much effort on the job at the expense of other parts of life is not a sure recipe for success and it can backfire badly. A manager may get some short-term benefit from stretching someone too far but in the long term everyone loses. It's not good for the individual, his family or your team. Chances are high that if someone is spending too much time at work, his personal life will suffer. It all spirals down from there.

"Work-life balance" and "work-life integration" are popular catchphrases these days. They refer to prioritizing your activities, managing the allocation of time for your work and personal life and setting boundaries between them. The objective is not to balance the hours one to one but to find the allocation that best meets all your needs.

This formula should take into account an individual's abilities, personality and the circumstances of her life. Some people really are focused more on their jobs than on other parts of their lives. Others think they have to force themselves to work more in order to get ahead. Sometimes an Underperformer may try to gain recognition and advancement just by devoting ever more time to the job. It can have a reverse effect.

The individual bears much of the load in setting these limits. However, it is well known that the culture of the workplace has a tremendous influence. As usual, the manager sets the framework by his own example. When you tell your employees that you don't want them to work long hours and you want them to have a full life outside of the job but then you come early, stay late and send them messages all night, you are giving them the opposite signal with your behavior. Guess which one carries more weight?

BOREDOM

It is a completely different situation when an employee or student is an Underperformer because of a basic lack of interest in her assigned tasks and responsibilities. When this happens, it is easy for her to lose sight of the importance of her work. It could be she has been assigned a job that is too easy. Maybe things got stale. Perhaps her manager is not sufficiently involved to inject fresh ideas and she has lost the motivation to make the effort to work at a high level. For whatever reason, the challenge that sparks interest is missing.

It is the manager's responsibility to realize this is happening, which again depends on staying in the fields with your people. The immediate step is to give the feedback that performance is not satisfactory. Typically, this works well if the message is delivered with some concrete suggestions for improvement.

NEW CHALLENGES

The obvious cure is to provide a new challenge. Boredom has shown up in my career and when it did, the only remedy for me was to find a new mission to inspire me. One time I actually took a break away from the company in order to force the issue that I needed a new challenge. I was pleased to return a few months later in a new position. My previous position was filled by a highly qualified individual who also was in need of a new role. In this case the organization benefited in multiple ways.

Perhaps you can work with a bored individual to unearth in him a new interest that matches a need of the team. Matching a skill he wants to develop in himself with a task that needs doing is the ideal. If this is not possible, you may have a mismatch on your hands.

TOSS A BISCUIT

Of course, it helps if you add some tangible benefits like money, promotion, increased responsibilities, a new smartphone or a biscuit. I have sometimes found that a carefully worded reference to the performance of others on the team may help to add a competitive aspect to the message. "Look at Stan and Jenny, they are really doing much better than we had anticipated and surely you are every bit as talented as those two."

Boredom is a particular hazard with an Outperformer, a Type that needs to be praised, rewarded and frequently challenged or he is likely to lose interest. If you put an Outperformer in a job that is not challenging, you are likely to see a quick drop-off in his performance. You must be careful not to place him in a role that minimizes the use of his talents or ignores his valuable contributions while burdening him with things that he is not really good at. When that happens, you will watch an Outperformer turn into an Underperformer right before your eyes.

MISMATCH

Poor performance in a job can be the result of putting someone in a role for which he simply is not suited. In such a case, the individual may have many strong abilities. The problem is a mismatch of those strengths with the job. The work may be too easy or too hard or call for a skill he doesn't possess or place him in an area about which he has no interest.

These mismatches are hard on the person and on the team. His particular abilities are not put to good use and needed functions are left uncompleted. It is unusual that someone will do well in a situation like this. Most usually, he will turn into an Underperformer.

A mismatch may appear to be a very slow transition to a new role, when in fact the individual is stuck on his journey over "the hump" and will never make it to the other side. In cases like this, after you've given feedback, encouragement and second chances, you will reach the point when you have to acknowledge poor performance.

NO AMBITION

Everyone cannot be The Best and I've learned there can be merits to being average. Sometimes a worker just wants to be a good producer and is not ambitious to advance. If that is the case and he is slotted into a new challenge, he can become discontent with the mismatch and soon turn into an Underperformer. I had an experience like this one time when I was asked to manage a business new to me. The firm chose me for this role because they needed someone who was a proven manager rather than someone with specialized knowledge of the business.

I found many of the people in the group were content to keep on doing things as usual, despite my efforts to get them to think outside of their comfort zone. They had a journeyman mindset and were reluctant to stretch themselves from it. Eventually I realized that this was okay because they were good enough at what they did and trying to make the changes was turning out to be counterproductive.

This experience reminded of the time a friend told me that I needed to realize my expectations for other people might not be the same as the expectations those people might have for themselves. This reprimand was handed to me more than 30 years ago and I call on it when I am evaluating someone I may incorrectly consider an underachiever.

I once had someone advocate that it's okay to just do the minimum amount of work required to collect a paycheck. I assume this person was also a C student. It can turn out this attitude can put you at risk of being the first to be let go when your employer is looking to reduce the work force.

On the other hand, I wonder if people who are satisfied with being average are generally happier with their lives. I wonder if I would still have hair if I had tried really hard to be average.

CAN'T ADAPT

Another kind of mismatch doesn't necessarily become evident just when someone takes on a new role. It can happen when the requirements of a job change over time and the individual does not adapt. I had an experience of this with two people who had done the same things for too long. They were both stuck in their ways and couldn't accept that they needed to change. They became Underperformers in denial, chained to the past and unable to adjust to the fact that the cheese had been moved. It was a long, difficult struggle to get them to see that they should move into other roles that were better suited to their skills.

Again, the manager's responsibility is to give the feedback. Then, together with the Underperformer, take the opportunity to analyze the reasons for the poor performance with the objective of finding a better match for him. I am always optimistic about this, when it is done honestly and genuinely, given my firm belief that there is a place for everyone.

LACK OF ABILITY

It is sometimes the case that someone in your care just isn't very talented and, no matter what measures you take, will not be able to perform at the level the job requires. This is the most extreme case of a mismatch. This is a fact of life and there are no management steps that can make it otherwise. The best strategy is to accept it when it is true. You can like the individual personally and wish things were otherwise but that will not change the poor performance.

Sometimes when inability is the problem, the individual may try to rely on personal relationships rather than merit to get ahead. He may go this route with the team and also with you as the manager. The technical term for this is "suck up." It sounds sort of sleazy and it is. I don't like to be sucked up to and I can usually smell it quickly. When it happens, I tend to want to ignore the person because I am embarrassed for him. Of course, because I know I have to give him the feedback, I tell him to cut it out. I say things like, "Stop climbing up my ass."

We all have known people who do this but they might not recognize themselves. It is a manager's, teacher's or parent's responsibility to identify the behavior and try to turn it in a different direction. I can see how sucking up might work to someone's benefit sometimes but I prefer actual hard work, thorough analysis and timely results. They win me over every time.

When those outcomes are not forthcoming, it may be time to accept that sometimes an Underperformer is just an Underperformer. Then it is time to look for a place where their lesser abilities and ambitions will be appreciated.

THE UNDERPERFORMER AS LEADER

Underperformers are not good at managing themselves. They certainly do not make good leaders. Don't do it.

THE UNDERPERFORMER
ADVICE SUMMARY

My best advice about how to manage the Type that is the Underperformer is to:

- Make them speak.
- Help them become self-aware.
- Give honest feedback that they are not performing as needed.
- Work with them to figure out the reason they are underachieving.
- Tend to outside issues.
- Check for boredom and take steps to introduce new challenges.
- Ensure a good match of skills and role.
- Recognize when you should seek a different place for them.

CHAPTER 13

THE ENTITLED –
MAKE HER SWEAT

TURKS AND CAICOS. I am attending a weeklong yoga retreat at an upscale resort on this beautiful island in the Caribbean. All of us attending it are happy to be working with the accomplished yoga teacher who is instructing us in our practice. This is a very comfortable and peaceful place.

I give you this information because having the ability to go to such nice places reminds me of how "entitled" I seem to have become in my adult life. This leads me to think of all those I have managed or worked with who had a sense of entitlement and how that made them major management challenges or even unemployable. Sometimes it seriously hindered their careers by making them unable to achieve sustainable success. It also reminds me of the disparity between this fancy resort and my fond memories of the "resort" known by my family as "Mrs. Crawford's."

WILDWOOD BY THE SEA

Reflecting on all those affluent, well bred and well-educated people I have managed, many of whom are now my friends and colleagues, makes me conjure their family beach compounds and the exclusive "waspy" islands where their families go year after year. It is in contrast to this that I recount how my family vacationed in Wildwood, New Jersey, every year and stayed in Mrs. Crawford's small, second floor efficiency apartment.

There were two tiny bedrooms. My parents slept in the room that had a full-sized bed while the four of us children shared the two single beds in the second room. It was all very simple and I suppose comfortable enough for kids between the ages of five and 14.

We always went to "Wildwood by the Sea" during the last two weeks in June, just after school ended, because those were the least expensive weeks of the summer for short-term rentals. There was no air conditioning, no pool and just a tiny bathroom and kitchenette.

I remember being so excited every evening after our walk on the boardwalk because we were then each allowed to purchase one food treat of our choice. Most of my siblings chose something sensible, like a slice of pizza, to be consumed and enjoyed immediately. But not me. I always wanted something that had lots of quantity – like pretzels or potato sticks – so I could "take an inventory" the next morning. I got more satisfaction from hoarding my fortune and celebrating it the next day than if I had chosen a hot dog or ice cream. Perhaps this was an early indication of my ability to forego immediate gratification in favor of a future goal.

THE ANOINTED

We all know the Type that I call the Entitled from our own lives and from books and movies. He goes around with his nose in the air or she is "stuck up" and unfriendly. She expects the lead role in the play. He refuses to do the boring practice drills with the rest of the team. This Type generally acts like they expect other people to do anything they say. The job for teachers, coaches, managers and other leaders is to find a way to make them see that others are equally worthy. In other words, cut them down to size and give them meaningful challenges.

I generally separate the Entitled into three main categories:

1. Those who went to the "right" schools.
2. Those who came from the "right" families.
3. Those who are "connected."

CHARACTERISTICS

These three groups share many of the same characteristics. The Entitled often tend to:

- Have an automatic sense of entitlement to the best projects, opportunities and success.
- Lack the hard-driving, sleeves-rolled-up, whatever-it-takes attitude that is necessary to learn from the bottom up.
- Be unable to work effectively as part of a team.

I have experienced the pedigreed individual who has been a great hardworking success but that has been the exception. I find most examples of this Type to be a management challenge, especially if they are new to the business world or have been moved to my group from some prior success within the firm.

I have an obvious bias given my background but I have often found that those I admire most – in my industry and other industries, both in the U.S. and globally – are those who got their position on their own merits and almost always without depending on family connections or a fancy education likely paid for by their parents.

The Entitled Type is pretty easy to spot in the interview process. If you don't pick up on it for some reason, they may be quick to let you know of their special status, especially when they keep bringing up the name of the elite school they went to – and they all do!

ALMA MATER

A successful CEO of a major global conglomerate once wrote how he would prefer to hire one person from a small state school who paid his own tuition rather than ten from an Ivy League school. It is no surprise that generally I agree with him. However, in a large organization, you don't always control who joins your team, your faculty or your brigade.

MISS IVY OXBRIDGE

One of my favorite stories about the Entitled is about a young summer intern who joined my group through my firm's recruiting program. She was from one of the most prestigious schools in the U.S. On the very first day, when this overly interviewed and exclusively selected "future star" made her debut on my trading desk, I gave her a task that involved working with spreadsheets. We all know that pretty much any college or even high school kid can work her way around a spreadsheet and often in a way resembling an orchestra conductor.

Well, this debutante looked up at me and in a mild huff said, "Oh, I go to Exclusive University and we don't learn or use Excel, so you will need to ask someone else to do this kind of work."

Can you imagine?

So I told my summer intern that perhaps she should spend the coming weekend learning a spreadsheet program because otherwise she would be on the next train back to Exclusive University. My team laughed for a week! She did learn a spreadsheet program quickly but things just got worse.

She refused to take the headphones out of her ears while working because she found everyone around her distracting. Did she not understand that she was working on a trading desk as an intern and that perhaps there were things to learn from those distracting people? One day, a very senior colleague asked her to work on a project for him and she responded, "Don't you have someone junior to do that for you?"

Ivy Oxbridge is a made-up name. Americans are familiar with the Ivy League schools but may not be aware that Ivy's last name, Oxbridge, is a well-known designation in Britain that means you attended either Oxford or Cambridge University. Being a graduate of the "right" school may be an even bigger issue in the U.K. than it is in the U.S.

Senior leaders I have known for years have worked to overcome this bias, especially those working for firms with a global reach. Still, many remain focused on the "right" school rather than the capability and experience of the candidates. The U.K. insiders' club (like the U. S. old boys' club) continues to play the system off the back of their little black books. People tell me this is changing but many of the people I interviewed in London, from several industries, affirm that this prejudice still exists more than most people think.

People with an elite education certainly can be valuable. I am just suggesting that this is not the way to evaluate them. I object to a prepaid ticket. Organizations need people with a diversity of skills and experience, including those gained as a result of having to work without the benefit of such advantages.

NOT PROPER

An American woman based in London told me how she had interviewed an impressive and experienced candidate for a possible position with her firm. She recognized how the candidate's strong communication skills and a proven track record of sales would make him a great match for a manager she knew who was looking for such people. When she recommended the candidate to the hiring manager, he glanced at the resume and promptly said that he couldn't consider the candidate because he didn't have a "proper" education.

Remember, this was not a recent graduate but someone with relevant experience! This happened in 2011. The firm needed people with these skills. I will never understand how you expect to survive in the global marketplace if you don't jump on the best candidates with proven experience.

This is an example of the reason I developed the technique I like to use when interviewing to fill a position where I have many people to consider for a relatively junior role. When I remove the name, school and outside activities from the resumes prior to giving them to the group of people who are working with me on the search, it is just amazing what happens.

As I sit by this beautiful pool waiting for my next three hours of yoga, I am still so thankful that 30 years ago I made it past this sort of test! For some reason, I am still surprised that this practice remains so blatant.

PEOPLE LIKE US

Another category of the Entitled Type is made up of those who come from the "right" family – one that is well known or has a pedigreed history or considerable wealth. In England, such people like to refer to themselves as "PLU" or "People Like Us." Doesn't it sound like some British costume drama?

When I started in the business world it was very commonplace that PLUs had advantages in getting good positions. One of my first managers was from a family with a name that would be familiar to the PLUs in a certain part of the U.S. He was one of those peculiar sorts who probably suffered from whatever it is you get when there has been too much interbreeding. I remember that he used to play "pocket ball" during meetings. We always wondered what it was he was looking for in there! It was 1982 and this was an Entitled guy who never paid for anything. He was always asking *me* for money to buy coffee or a cigar.

One day, just before we were all leaving for the Christmas holidays, he called me to his desk and started fumbling in those pockets. I was getting a little uncomfortable but like any lowly analyst, I respectfully waited. Out of his pockets came a wad of wrinkled dollar bills. He threw them on his desk and then gathered a single five-dollar bill and ten singles.

He handed them to me and said, "Here, this is for you. Maybe you can save some money and go to college one day." I figured that to him I was just some kid from the street who got lucky. At least he got that right!

RIGHT FAMILY

I am happy to say that coming from the "right" family no longer matters in terms of advancement or promotion in most industries. Organizations would be foolish not to promote and reward whoever can make them successful, especially in our intensely globally competitive environment. While it is great that this is rarely a requirement when it comes to advancement, it is still very prevalent when it comes to getting introduced to the right people if you are junior. Family connections still open doors.

In my experience, the results of this practice are mixed. It becomes pretty clear that there is a problem when the individual doesn't show up regularly or insists on letting everyone know that he is from a Right Family. What gets tricky is when Mr. Right really isn't working out and he has Papa or Mama Right complaining to senior management. I do believe that this is becoming less of an issue, at least in the U. S., though it still holds sway in the U. K.

SOC AND DOC

The third category that makes up the Entitled Type includes those who get special opportunities as a result of being "connected" in some way. Typically, this connection is to a company's important client or to a nonprofit organization's significant donor. These people can be offspring or a distant relative, a friend or even a neighbor. For many years I have referred to these fortunate people as SOC (Son of Client) and DOC (Daughter of Client).

CONNECTIONS

Clearly, working your connections to help your children get opportunities to succeed is natural and appropriate. The challenge for managers and organizations is to balance granting the requests for these opportunities with finding the right place to put these people, while continuing to manage their businesses. I have been involved in these situations many times over the last 30 years and my experience has been extreme at both ends: It can be a huge success or a total disaster.

In all cases, the success stories have involved individuals who I could tell had strong role models in their development. Each of them had most of the qualities that I recommended you look for when hiring, namely, a willingness to do whatever is asked, respect and, tellingly, an attitude of "un-entitled."

READ THE MANUAL

I remember one young guy who was the son of a very significant client of my firm. I remember once having a discussion with him when he told me how his father required him and his siblings to read completely through the instruction manual for any new toy, TV or other technology they were given. He told me that they weren't even allowed to have the item until the manual was read.

This parental discipline was clearly reflected in his work. He had a strong command of detail that was especially important when we were under pressure. He was also a good team player, a natural teacher and an all around nice guy. I never once heard this fellow mention his close connection to one of the firm's largest clients.

GIVE THEM A CHANCE

Once, just after the conclusion of a disastrous situation with a SOC elsewhere in the firm, I was asked to take on a new DOC. I knew I had developed a reputation for handling these situations well and that other managers felt confident I would give such people a real chance to succeed. I always have provided them with a platform to learn, the right mentor and even sufficient rope for hanging themselves.

In this latest case, I refused to hire the DOC unless she went through the interview process with many members of my team. I did not let my team know of the actual situation but told them that if we all agreed we liked her, we would have her join us for one year. I told my group that she had been hired for a role in a different part of our firm and needed some training with us first. Their feedback was that they didn't know what the candidate would do, given her limited experience, but everyone was sure the DOC would work real hard. This made me pretty confident that she would turn out just fine.

My group's endorsement made me interested to learn more. After my interview with her, the reason for their positive view was clear to me as well. She was totally prepared, serious, modest and yet confident. This DOC never once made mention of any connection or special affiliation. She told me about how desperate she was to find affordable housing and how she had driven her own belongings to New York City in a rented truck. This alone told me tons. I knew her parents could have bought the truck company and probably an entire building in Manhattan to house their daughter. My gut told me that this woman understood that she would have to "do whatever it takes" to earn her place on our team.

Not only did this DOC succeed, she thrived. We quickly determined that we wanted her to be a permanent member of our group and I abandoned the pretense that this was a temporary situation. When someone on the team left, we gave her a permanent position. She continues to thrive.

DELINQUENTS

The yogic me would prefer just to focus on the positive stories, but you do need to know what happens when the SOC, DOC or FOC (Friend of Client) placement does not work out so well. The reasons for this are typically pretty straightforward. These individuals have such feelings of entitlement that they just don't think they need to work very hard. They have pretty much had most things handed to them for their whole lives and usually they want to make sure everyone knows that they "deserve" some protective status.

I had such a one working on one of my teams who just didn't think he needed to show up much of the time. This SOC frequently let people know of his "connection" and when in the office he was often difficult to find. No surprise that he did little work or took forever to get his assignments done. When he did claim that something was finished, the results were poor. He also regularly let everyone know which parts of his role he considered to be beneath him and the few things that he did find interesting, most of which were beyond his knowledge or experience level.

Typically, these situations eventually result in a call from the client to the senior management of the firm to complain that junior is not being challenged. These calls are extremely common and that's not surprising because the parent has likely been making these sorts of calls for junior's whole life.

The best you can do in these circumstances is to keep good documentation on junior so that if things get ugly and you need to manage him out of your team, you can substantiate your position. You should also then be praying that junior either gets fed up and quits or expresses a strong interest in doing something outside of your purview. If that happens, be sure to give your colleagues a heads up with an honest assessment of junior's attitude and abilities, so they can approach him with eyes wide open.

In this story the SOC resigned but not without trying to take down a few of my people with him. This is another reminder of the importance of staying close to your people. I knew the real story and I had documentation to prove it.

STAR POWER

A variation on being connected is to have some form of star power. Think of how often you read about college sports stars getting off without going to class and yet getting passing grades. Even worse is when the sibling of a smart student or sports star at your school gets preferential treatment because of an assumption that the family connection means the next sibling will be just as talented as the older child.

SPORTS CONNECTION

About 20 years ago, corporations urged men to avoid using sports analogies when talking business in an effort to be more inclusive of what was by then becoming a diverse population of colleagues. Please accept my apologies for using sports to illustrate this kind of connection!

A retired army general told me a story about a ranking officer who had filled one of his most senior positions. The new chap came with glowing references from other senior officers and years' worth of outstanding performance reviews. Not long after he assumed his new role, it became pretty clear that things were not working out. The various mid-level officers began to falter and the unit began to lose its organizational strength. Further research into the new leader's background showed that during most of his early years of service, this guy had been a cricket star and a major figure on several other sports teams as well. It seems his athletic and scoring abilities were mistakenly understood to indicate that he had skills at leadership. There was actually little evidence that he had ever really performed well when playing the position of senior officer.

The general quickly moved to correct this situation. As he did, many high-ranking officers told him that this could not be done. He did it anyway, replacing Joe Jock with someone who had less stellar credentials but a proven reputation for effective management of large groups. It all worked out beautifully from there.

BAD MANNERS

Another version of star power is when someone adopts a superior and condescending manner in an attempt to leverage his relationship with someone of elevated status. In this case, this Entitled Type fills his head with images of being a senior member of the organization and interacts with others unsuitably. Sometimes he mimics the manner and attitudes of his boss, insensitive to its inappropriateness.

I remember once being in a meeting where I was one of about a dozen very senior managers who had come together to discuss an issue and make a decision about it. One of my peers was unable to attend and sent someone in her place. This relatively young person introduced himself and then proceeded to speak to everyone in the room as if he, himself, were his super senior leader. He adopted her demeanor of authority in the way he spoke and went on as though he had 25 years' more experience than he did. It was inappropriate and offensive and even embarrassing, although he did not realize it.

As it turned out, it was much worse than just his behavior. Although he had come with the affect of his boss, he was there without her decision-making authority. The next day, he delivered a message to us from her about the decision we had reached in our meeting. When he had checked with her about it, her reply was, "I've agreed to nothing."

This was a costly waste of time for a senior group like that and did not sit well with me or the other meeting participants. I resolved that if that guy ever spoke to me like that again, I would walk out of the room. I learned afterward that this fellow had a history of acting like this. I spoke with a colleague in Texas who had had a similar experience with him.

He said he told the fellow, "If you ever talk to me like that again, I'm going to fly up there to New York City and punch you in the face."

Another Texas colleague who had also known him acknowledged that he had also seen the same behavior. "But," he said, "he's not so bad once you get to know him." Faint praise!

The question for his senior manager is: Why send your delegate if you are giving him no authority? She accepted this as good feedback and said she passed it on to him. Did she revise her ability to truly delegate?

REVERSAL OF FORTUNE

I remember times when I have managed people like this and had to work really hard to help them undo this kind of behavior. One of these had previously worked for several very demanding and pushy (but successful) leaders. This twenty-something had assumed the speaking style and the demanding, Entitled stance of her previous managers. It was a disaster in her new role.

Within reason, proven leaders or managers who are able consistently to attract, retain and mentor talent can act however they wish, provided they remember one thing. They need to make sure that they are not creating monsters in their own image.

Just as children and students learn attitudes and behaviors from their parents, teachers and coaches, junior people learn matters of style from their managers. Promising young stars should be careful which of their leader's traits they adopt when interacting with their employees, colleagues and especially with people who are senior to them. Some of these behaviors just are not suitable for someone of their more limited experience. They may find their aspirations for the future cut short, delayed or redirected to some other path.

Sometimes it is possible to correct this; other times it is not. The most important message to the senior leader or mentor is that you need to make sure such behavior is discouraged. If you don't, you are doing a disservice to your younger ones.

THE ENTITLED AS LEADER

There are plenty of reasons an Entitled individual may find himself in a leadership position. In some cases, it comes with the territory in the sense that an employer may want to please a client by advancing the SOC or DOC or FOC. This is generally a worst-case reason to make someone a manager from the point of view of the well being of the team and even the business.

On the other hand, someone who is Entitled and also has a can-do attitude and qualities of good performance and teamwork can make as good a manager as anyone else. Moving such a person into a management position can make great sense. This is especially attractive if, in addition to showing himself a good leader, he can attract new business from his own connections.

THAT'S LIFE

The Entitled will always be a factor in whatever it is that you do. There will always be preferential treatment for some, for reasons other than their abilities, whether money, family, education or connections. This will always be at the expense of others. It is best to accept this at the outset.

As the manager of someone with a fancy degree or a family connection or star power, the most valuable thing you can do is to make that individual recognize that, despite his status, he still has to do his job and earn his success.

When you guide a successful Entitled individual to become a leader, do be on the lookout that he doesn't give preferential treatment to others of the Entitled Type. Sometimes this will be a struggle for him because of powerful lifelong conditioning. Other times, with your help, he will develop sensitivity to the issue.

What I believe, what I have seen and what I have enjoyed is that things can work out well when the Entitled individual chooses to focus on excellence and on building her own strengths over a sustained period.

There will be plenty of times when things don't happen that way. The Entitled have their own version of denial and will often reject criticism because they are so firm in their beliefs about their "specialness." The Entitled Type is also quite prone to take on the stance of the Lone Ranger. They may do this as a way of pushing that entitlement around by striking out on their own without regard to the team. On the other hand, under their veneer of entitlement they may be insecure about their abilities and follow the route of the Underperformer when he goes off on his own.

When the Entitled individual makes trouble, the manager's most important job is to take steps to minimize the disruption to the team. In most cases, you must remain discreet about the issue and there may be limits to what you can do to remedy the situation. Nevertheless, with some creativity you can search out a way to separate the problem from the good work and development of the rest of the group.

THE ENTITLED

ADVICE SUMMARY

My best advice about how to manage the Type that is the Entitled is to:

- Accept that the Entitled will always be a factor. That's life.
- Focus on excellence and building strengths.
- Remind them that they, too, have to work hard to earn their stripes.
- Stay close to your people in order to be aware of the realities.
- Manage them out when they get in the way of progress.
- Be discreet to minimize disruption to the overall team but don't ignore difficult situations.

CHAPTER 14

THE FLUFFER – DON'T BE FOOLED

REMOTE-IN-HAND, NEW YORK. I live in a state of addiction to home shopping television. I think of it as a form of meditation, like watching moving wallpaper. One thing I find fascinating is how the people selling the items on these channels can spend an entire 10 minutes discussing something as mundane as an eyebrow pencil or a screwdriver set. Or 30 minutes or an hour or more talking and talking about a fancy high-speed food blender or a trendy designer pocketbook. They make every product sound so compelling! They make us believe that everything they say must be true!

They are so convincing in their descriptions and explanations of a product that you find you want to buy it. It's easy to see why this is a $10 billion dollar global business.

The ability of the presenters to generate so many words about one item is amazing. These are people who know how to use the art of talking to influence behavior. They make me think of the Type that I call the Fluffer.

A Fluffer is a performer, a smooth talker who is skilled at putting a spin on almost anything but then may not come through. There are several varieties of Fluffer but they all share one outstanding quality: above all else a Fluffer is a great communicator.

COMMUNICATION SKILLS MATTER!

I believe that having strong communication skills is more important than the ability to do good work. I see evidence of this almost every day. The two central, most important things about the topic of fluffing are:

1. If someone is a great communicator but otherwise has only marginally effective abilities, he can still have a very successful career. As long as he can talk a good game, he will do well.

2. Conversely, the reality is that someone can be super smart and really good at what he does but if he can't communicate well, he'll never get as far as he should.

Being a good communicator does not mean someone is a Fluffer. When a Fluffer also has substance, it is a winning combination and the individual can be a strong performer. Outperformers who are great communicators are pretty fortunate.

I can't repeat too often my single, strongest recommendation to parents, teachers, coaches, managers and leaders of all kinds to promote and encourage the learning and strengthening of communication skills. Tell your children, students and developing employees to:

- Take acting classes
- Join debate clubs
- Practice, practice, practice!

FLUFFERS ARE EVERYWHERE

We can find a Fluffer everywhere in our lives. As kids, we may have known him as the class clown. He was often popular because he could always find something to say and could be entertaining. Sometimes you'd find yourself wondering about her answer in class but you could count on her to speak up and she'd always come up with something. He was great at talking up his performance on the swim team, regardless how well he actually swam. She could be very frustrating as a friend when she didn't come through with what she said she'd do.

For parents, teachers, coaches, managers and other leaders, the challenge is to find the way to cut through all the words and to deal directly with the substance.

FAILURE TO DELIVER

The Fluffer's skill can be super useful depending on how it is used and on expectations. However, the fast talkers with no substance and no follow through eventually struggle, fail or, as adults, shift from job to job.

The problems with the Fluffer arise when he speaks with authority but doesn't have the skills to back it up. A Fluffer can be knowledgeable and yet unable to create an action plan out of what he knows. He uses talk as a substitute for a plan. More often than not, a Fluffer does not have the ability to say, "I don't know."

CHARACTERISTICS

The characteristics of the Fluffer are that they tend to:

- Be great talkers and persuaders but do not know how to manage a project or a team.
- Be generally unable to work with detail.
- Frequently fail to deliver desirable results.

It is extremely difficult to identify Fluffers in the interview process. Their great speaking skills equip them to excel in interviews and it is generally only when you are working with them day to day that you begin to notice the problems. Just always try to be aware that you could be getting fluffed. If you do suspect this is happening in an interview, press for specifics and pay close attention to what you hear.

FLUFFER VARIETIES

Fluffers come in several varieties.

- **Smooth Talker**: This is a compelling speaker who sells himself into a management role that requires skills beyond his expert "performances." This kind is a good salesperson but then things crumble quickly as the business around him weakens and the team loses its footing due to his lack of leadership. These Fluffers use their communication skills to divert your attention. Often they put their efforts into spending "face time" with others to talk up their cause rather than doing the actual work. They typically are so seduced by their ongoing articulation of their own brilliance that they figure they can survive whatever disturbances might be going on around them.

- **Manage-Upper**: This is a manager who is good at articulating the details of her business without actually grasping their meaning and their implications. Above all, she is skilled at spinning reports to upper management that make it appear that she is delivering results.
- **Yes-Boss Parrot**: A variation of the Manage-Upper is the Fluffer who always agrees with his boss. He typically uses somewhat different words to make it appear that what he heard from his superior is his own thinking. His managers do not have visibility into the lack of foundation in this person's area of responsibility. As a result, a skilled Yes-Boss Parrot can have a long reign. This can lead to a longer-term disaster as things keep deteriorating underneath the spin, resulting in damage to the business and the team.
- **User**: This is someone who uses other people to make herself appear smart and effective. She may appropriate others' work as her own, communicate their efforts as if they are the result of her management influence or report on work to which she was only marginally connected.
- **Bagger**: Beware of the Fluffer as a "Bagger." This is someone who uses fluffing to sell a colleague something undesirable. Think "double-cross." I had an experience of this once when a senior woman colleague came to me to try to sell me an under-achiever. She painted an amazingly wonderful picture of this guy. What she didn't know is that he had been a summer MBA intern of mine and that we had recommended to the review committee that the firm not hire him. However, the firm did and my colleague inherited him when she took over a business unit. Now she was aware of his limitations

and wanted to move him out. After she finished her endorsement and recommendation that I was the best person to challenge this individual, I dropped the bomb of my knowledge about him. She turned beet red. Fluffer as Bagger. Gotcha!

MANAGING FLUFFERS

If you stay in the fields with your people, you will be better able to notice when you have a Fluffer on your hands. Spending time with him one-on-one to discuss the details of his work gives you the chance to unearth the absence of substance.

WHEN IT WORKS

When you find yourself with a Fluffer on your team, you need to keep your eye on him. If you recognize this tendency in someone who is early in his career, you have the opportunity to correct this behavior. Be on your toes to challenge him immediately and directly when he appears to be fluffing. The recommendation I make to "listen, just shut up and say something" becomes especially important for this Type. Press him to provide details substantiating what he is saying. Stay on top of him to come through in his work responsibilities. Sit hard on him for metrics and benchmarks.

When a Fluffer develops those abilities and also builds solid management skills, he can use them in combination with his natural talents at communication to excel as a leader. Most people will find better success when they communicate well and this Type has a huge advantage in that regard. This also applies to children, students, salespeople or team leaders.

WHEN IT DOESN'T WORK

If your Fluffer doesn't take your guidance, your next choice is to place her in a position that matches her strengths. There is nothing wrong with a skill set that is based on good communication. It can be a very positive and desirable attribute. People who are good at it can often turn out to be phenomenal salespeople and can be motivating speakers. In this case, it is good management to move your Fluffer to a job where those skills are an asset. This challenge is similar to the one you have with Outperformers who do not make good leaders: you must manage expectations. Help her accept what she is good at and help her find a way to be rewarded for it.

The problem with the Fluffer Type arises when someone pretends she is something she is not. If she buys into her own story and you call her on it, then denial can become a factor. When that happens, her skewed idea of herself as super successful and her misperception of her own abilities can lead her to become quite disruptive.

There is a Fluffer version of the Lone Ranger Type, who widely broadcasts her greatness and then fails to help the team do its work. When she falsely claims abilities she lacks, she can cause problems that damage the group effort. As long as she thinks she's getting away with her sham, she will keep on promoting herself. When her pretense is finally discovered, she can find herself tumbling hard.

SHOWMAN

Many Fluffers can be wonderful actors but don't want to deal with details in any fashion. One example was a fellow who was hired for a job with two roles: to talk to clients about strategy and to manage a business. The reality was, he was exclusively a showman with very little capacity below the surface. He was great at talking about the strategy but terrible at managing the business. He didn't even pretend to know the details. It was pretty easy to detect this and to move him out of the role.

Remember the story about hiring someone after 40 interviews, only to have to let him go a short time later? That was a story about a Fluffer and it highlights the difficulty of dealing with this kind of performer. The person in question was articulate, friendly, fun, attractive, polished, well dressed and had good credentials. He was aggressive in selling his abilities during his interviews.

Once he got to work on the job, it turned out he was all talk and no ability. He couldn't make a decision about even simple things. He did not apply common sense. He could not meet a deadline. He regularly escalated matters to senior management unnecessarily. In some cases, he was not honest. In many cases, he may have been fooling himself into thinking everything was going okay or thought the fact that something was under way was good enough, when an actual outcome was what was required. Gradually things fell apart and the truth behind the scenes was uncovered.

FLUFFERS AS COLLEAGUES

To me, having a colleague who is a Fluffer is the hardest Fluffer situation to deal with. Such a colleague will make promises easily and you have to come to learn she will never keep them. The things you depend on her for do not happen. Frequently, she will get recognition for accomplishments that are not hers.

You know your colleague is a Fluffer when you hear her spouting the ideas you recognize from your own conversations with others and when the generalities outpace the specifics. Another tip-off is her use of an overwhelming volume of words that leave you scratching your head looking for meaning.

PUSHY

Sometimes you encounter someone who is a Fluffer by force of his personality or position. He may have been around the business for a long time and be valued for his store of institutional memory and his deep knowledge of the industry. He is aggressive in taking control of the conversation, overrides others' comments and shuts out other people's thoughts. Everyone is cowed by him and meekly waits to hear what he will say. He announces decisions and does not explain the reasoning behind them.

He is often right, but he does not engage his colleagues in the matter at hand, so no one actually knows his thinking or the rationale for what they are asked to do. This is fluffing as a bullying technique. It can be very tiring to work with a colleague of this Type. It makes you want to leave your job.

OXYGEN BURGLARS

I remember being part of a management team made up of 12 people. I also remember that in our meetings most of these individuals felt like they needed to speak on every topic. Usually, the first person summarized the issue sufficiently. Yet all the others seemed to think that they had to talk as well. Most of them added nothing. This is an example of fluffing in order to get public recognition. I like to refer to these people as "oxygen burglars."

THE FLUFFER AS LEADER

I had a boss for about five years who was a Fluffer. He used to assemble many people at endless meetings where he would talk at great length about his ideas. Almost always when we left these performances, the audience would ask each other, "Exactly what is it that we are to do now?" He provided no detail and no clear direction.

DELEGATORS

There are circumstances when a Fluffer can be a very successful manager. This requires that he have self-awareness about his shortcomings as well as his strengths and it usually rests on his being able to delegate well.

This Type can be quite good at discussing the business on a general level and frequently use a "pass along" technique, where they articulate positioning statements and high-level strategies. But when it comes to the nuts-and-bolts details of implementation and to techniques for how to manage a team, they are weak.

To compensate, a Fluffer who is a good leader has the wisdom to delegate the work of figuring out how to implement the ideas he is so good at expressing. He assigns that work to a few key people and creates a team to manage the implementation. Along with this, he puts in place a strong reporting system so he can stay on top of things.

As the team keeps him informed, he can represent the details of the business, even though his hands-on connection to them is slight. This way, he can appear to be both a good manager and a good speaker. This can be good for the manager and for the ones he delegates to and for the project and for the firm. These managers may have very big jobs and attract a lot of praise.

SMOKE AND MIRRORS

Other times, the Fluffer just relies on talking a good game. He acts like a salesman but has nothing to sell. I recall one instance when such a manager was required to have his team take over complex matters to which he paid no attention. He kept up a pretense that he was running the business and no one ever checked him. Only when serious errors were exposed did it become apparent that he was not doing the job, even though the high-level statistics and metrics he had provided had showed otherwise.

In another case, the Fluffer never bothered with the pretense. She was a great communicator and terrible at managing. She just stuck to putting on a show. It didn't take long for the problems to surface and she was moved to a different role.

TRANSLATOR

I knew one manager who was skilled at taking a message from his superior about something that needed to happen and then turning it into his own words. He assigned his team to deal with the specifics necessary to get the work done. While he had the right message and was good at delegating, he was not good at holding the team accountable because he himself did not understand the details about what needed to happen.

In one high-profile case, his task was to cut costs and headcount. He did this and looked like a hero. Then it turned out he had done it without sensitivity to the impact of those specific cuts on the business. He had cut out the middle staff, keeping the top managers and the lower support people. This had the desired impact on the budget. However, by doing it this way, he lost the people who really knew the business and in time the business suffered badly. So did he.

THE FLUFFER
ADVICE SUMMARY

My best advice about how to manage the Type that is the Fluffer is to:

- Encourage someone who is a great communicator, because he can have a very successful career regardless of his other abilities.
- Be aware that even if someone is really smart and productive, if he can't communicate well, he may never get as far as he should.
- Urge children, students and employees to learn and strengthen communication skills. Tell them to take acting classes, join debate clubs, and practice, practice, practice!
- Spend one-on-one time with the Fluffer to challenge him and press him to do the work.
- Place Fluffers who are strong communicators in jobs where those skills are valuable.

CHAPTER 15

THE BULLY -
SCHOOLYARD REDUX

PHILADELPHIA, PA. I was bullied regularly as a kid growing up in Philadelphia. My peers in school and in the neighborhood bullied me and I had to plan which streets I could walk down, thinking about where there would be kids waiting to beat me up or chase me or call me names. Worse, I was bullied by teachers at my school and by other adults in my life, as a child and a teenager.

TOUGH TO SHAKE

The experience of being bullied while growing up never goes away. People who were bullied as children carry the scars forever and it colors their responses throughout life. They are conditioned to be super sensitive to conflict and personal confrontation. They can have big problems with negative feedback and disapproval. They can have heightened reactions to hostility and antagonistic behavior, to disagreement, even to simple unfriendliness. Their reactions to these things can be emotionally charged.

IT'S EVERYWHERE

Bullying happens everywhere and not just with children and not just in school. There is bullying in the adult world too. It happens at home and at work and in many social contexts. It happens to spouses, partners, colleagues and employees.

It is quite common to find the Type that I call the Bully in the workplace. It is important to be able to recognize when bullying is happening and to understand the impact it can have on the success of our organizations and the health of our relationships.

YOU KNOW THEM

Most of us know this Type from childhood, whether we ourselves were bullied or only saw it happening to others. Maybe we even did it ourselves. Remember how, when I was a kid "playing business" at home, I used to make my sister sit for hours at that little plastic table outside my door as my secretary? That was an instance of bullying, as she is quick to point out!

Bullies are after power in one way or another in order to get advantages for themselves and that generally means putting someone else down. The Bully is the one who shouts to get her way. He may have grown big before his classmates and uses his size to get others to do what he wants. If she doesn't have physical size, she may develop a way of taking up a lot of space with her movements along with her loud voice. He may use taunts to make someone else feel bad. She may make fun of girls who are not part of her circle.

The challenge for parents, teachers, coaches, managers and leaders of all kinds is to spot it and stop it. There's no lack of opportunity, as there is pretty much always a Bully Type around, or several, in any organization.

CHARACTERISTICS

While bullying can take several forms, the usual characteristics of this Type are that they tend to:

- Be arrogant and aggressive.
- Ridicule others.
- Use their voice or physical presence to intimidate.

Sometimes this Type is just a cocky tough guy and that's the way he learned to live in the world. Perhaps he believes that he can get ahead only by scaring others off or intimidating or making fun of them. Beyond this, I believe Bullies are often insecure in their own abilities and their reaction is to put someone else down. I think this also happens when a Bully is envious of someone else's progress and, because of this, turns venom against him.

INTOLERANCE

There are other forms of bullying besides direct ridicule and badgering. One of these is intolerance of people who are different. This Bully strikes out with a knee-jerk reaction of feeling "better than" other people and taking action to put them "in their place."

An example of this happened with me last year when a colleague heard I was preparing to leave on a trip to India to an Ashram-style yoga retreat. She said, "You are not normal." This same person then asked in a disparaging tone if I were "turning Hindu." That kind of judgmental intolerance about something another person does is a kind of bullying. And that's not even to mention the small-minded prejudice behind a comment like that.

TUNNEL VISION

Sometimes this kind of behavior happens because of lack of experience. Some Bullies don't know any better because that's what they have seen, and been taught, their whole lives. These people say, "Because that's the way we do it." And it's up to all the rest of us to say, "Don't give me that crap!"

The Entitled can be Bullies too. Their assumptions about being "better than" others can lead them to treat others badly.

Bullying also shows up in Fluffers. When a Fluffer shifts into gear talking a hot streak or talks over you or doesn't let anyone else talk, he is being a Bully. So is the Bagger Fluffer when she pulls out her tricks to try to take advantage of you.

It's generally difficult to spot a Bully in the interview process. Perhaps you will notice a manner of bravado or arrogance in your conversation. You will do well to check about it with others who are also doing the interviewing. This may be a time to trust your gut feeling.

BEWARE! BE AWARE!

Being aware that bullying is happening gives you better control over your reactions. The victim of bullying may be conditioned to retreat or to lash out with outsized anger or even to bully back. None of these responses is productive.

From time to time over the years, I have felt bullied in my professional life. Sometimes this feeling is real and I am in fact being bullied. Other times, I know that I react as if I am being bullied when in reality I am not. When you are bullied as a child, it can be a continuous struggle as an adult to avoid the reflex of emotions that kick in when things happen that echo those early experiences. I find that some circumstances just bring back all the feelings and reactions that I had when I was bullied as a kid.

Getting a good grip on the reality of the situation, in addition to your emotional sense of it, will help you cut off the Bully's power. It can even help you to recognize when it is not a bullying situation after all. Sometimes those reactions can be mismatched to the reality of the circumstances.

WAS I BULLIED?

At one point not long ago, I had a pretty serious disagreement with my manager and I had a powerful, angry reaction. I thought a lot about it and realized that the situation had triggered old emotions that were familiar from my being browbeaten and harassed in the schoolyard and the neighborhood.

Realizing this let me sort out what was happening and address the actual reality of our encounter. I went to my manager and talked it over. I still didn't agree with him but I knew I was dealing with a legitimate disagreement, not a Bully.

WAS SOMEONE ON MY TEAM BULLIED?

I am particularly challenged when others don't recognize an individual's merit or an accomplishment that I feel warrants praise, promotion or some other reward. I am never proud of how I react to this and it has been a struggle for me for many years. My mental process escalates into mild rage, then sleeplessness and constant analysis of the scenario. This is no different than what happens when a parent thinks the teacher, school or coach is treating her child unfairly.

I have spent lots of time "analyzing" why my reaction can be so strong. I believe that, as a souvenir of my childhood bullying, I have a strongly developed reflex of wanting to correct a perceived "injustice." It is a constant struggle for me, but as a "yogi" I honor that challenge.

MANAGING BULLIES

Understanding that bullying is not just a school-age phenomenon helps a leader be alert to Bully behavior that may be taking place in his group and to stop it. This goes beyond watching for shouting and noisy confrontation.

Badgering, negatively criticizing or making fun of people who do not perform as expected or are different in some way are all harmful actions. None of it helps others to improve their performance. More likely it will inflict scars. It is a form of bullying and teachers, parents, coaches, managers and leaders all need to be aware of their own attitudes about this.

It can be difficult to detect bullying between peers if no one alerts the manager to the behavior. My best way of dealing with this is by sticking with my often-repeated advice that managers, teachers and leaders of all kinds need to be in the fields to stay close to their people.

COMPETITOR OR BULLY?

At the same time, the manager needs to be able to make a distinction between the behavior of someone who is being a Bully and that of someone who happens to be highly competitive. The latter can be aggressive at times and stick out his elbows to get an edge. However, I have found that competitive people tend to be more team oriented and often have a higher level of skills and knowledge than a Bully.

Competitive people are more likely to really want to do the right thing and in general are less offensive. If you're not sure, stay tuned to your gut feeling. Remember that each individual, even if competitive, needs positive support and encouragement to improve and excel.

ACT FAST

A subtle and mean-spirited form of bullying happens when a manger, teacher or parent knowingly puts someone into a role that is not matched to his talents. When this happens, he is set up to fail. He is open to being criticized or ridiculed and to other forms of bullying.

One of the big responsibilities of the manager is to help make sure that people work on the things they can improve and to be sure that conditions are right for that improvement to happen. When they spot a bullying interaction among their students, children, employees and colleagues, and know how to assess and manage it quickly, they can cut it off and let everyone move ahead.

THE BULLIED ONE BECOMES THE BULLY

I am also aware of the reality that those who are bullied can become Bullies themselves. I suspect that from time to time I have been guilty of this as well. As you know, I am a strong proponent of giving immediate feedback, whether positive or negative. When it is negative (or "constructive" as I see it), I am told it can feel harsh to the ones receiving it. Maybe they think they are being bullied when this happens and I have had people who reacted as if that were the case.

In general, though, I am told that the feedback, while it may sting, is helpful. In large part, this is because the people receiving it know it is given with good intention and as a way to help them develop and grow. Clarifying the intention behind strong behaviors is central to determining if it is bullying.

THE BULLY AS LEADER

It is a gruesome thought to consider the Bully in a management position. This Type tends to "lead" by using aggression and intimidation. If your boss is a Bully, your best option may be to breathe, keep calm and keep notes to document your experience. You can use this when you find your opportunity to confront him to insist on better treatment. It usually takes a pretty strong character to pull this off.

If the people the Bully manages are insecure in their jobs, they may have to find ways to put up with his tactics. However, a team that fears its leader is unlikely to do good work and its members will most assuredly look for ways to find different positions. When their Bully manager discovers this, retribution and punishment may ensue. For the people in his group, the dread just builds.

It won't help matters when the faulty performance of the group reflects back on the leader in the eyes of his peers. This can put his own job in jeopardy and that will often lead him to redouble his antagonism and dish out reprisals. It is an unpleasant cycle with one clear lesson: don't make a Bully a leader.

BEING "TUFF"

I've had a few leaders bully me from time to time. One notable example came when a new boss was drop-shipped into my business from a different part of the firm. He had a deep understanding of the overall industry but knew less about our specific area. He brought with him quite the reputation for toughness and we quickly saw that his reputation appeared to be well deserved. At the time of his arrival, I was already in a senior leadership position.

One of my first glimpses of this person's bullying tendencies came early on, when a colleague and I were berated for not understanding the daily frequency with which our new leader wanted telephone updates. Late in the afternoon of a particularly volatile day in the financial markets, he called both of us into his office, raised his voice to a thunderous roar and complained that we were not timely enough in giving him the updates.

His way of communicating this was to shout, "Do I speak Chinese? DO I SPEAK CHINESE?"

For more than a few moments, I considered asking, "Well, I did hear that you speak five languages so maybe one of them is Chinese?" However, I did think better of it and didn't say that out loud. I thought it would have been great to see his reaction!

Over time, I did realize that, although he was a very demanding manager, he wasn't unreasonable. He actually helped to sharpen some of my skills. I came to recognize this only after many unpleasant interactions, one of which became the tipping point.

One morning I arrived late to the office and was greeted by a group of my employees telling me that Bully Boss had repeatedly called, for more than two hours, demanding to speak with me and refusing to talk to anyone but me. I especially remember a small, usually meek woman colleague urgently telling me that the guy was "apoplectic" that I hadn't returned his calls.

I immediately went to his office. As usual, he was sitting at his desk. Whenever you went to his office, he always sat behind his desk and had you sit across the room on a sofa that was significantly lower in height.

As I sat down across the room, he began yelling, "Don't you know you have to be available when I need you and not make me wait?"

He repeated this several times and then, still sitting, he screamed, "Don't you know that when I call you I expect you to be there?" As he bellowed, he hit the desk telephone with his extended finger to emphasize each word. It was fierce and loud.

Without a second of hesitation, I stood up, walked over to his desk and jabbed my own finger on his phone. I matched his tone and said, "Don't you think by now I understand what it means when you need something from me?"

Heatedly I continued, "I'm late because my dog is dying and I am sure that is of no interest to you. Don't you understand yet the way I run my team? There are several people in my group perfectly qualified to answer your questions, perhaps even better than I can!"

To my surprise, suddenly he was no longer a Bully. He sat back and laughed like Hannibal Lecter as he said, "I knew one day you would come back at me because I knew you were tuff." That's how he said it: "tuff." Clearly, he had been waiting for and expecting this moment.

From that day on, his behavior toward me was completely different. He treated me more like a colleague and there was almost no more bullying. I believe he was just testing me and waiting to see if I would push back. Once he saw my own strength, he stopped.

I suppose you could sometimes think of a bullying attitude as a technique for a leader to find out someone's character. You'll need to use your judgment and your gut instinct to decide if that's what's happening. If it is, I think it's worth it to push back at least once. You may benefit by gaining self-confidence and hopefully some respect from the Bully.

OUTING BULLIES

Unfortunately, there is a general failure of adults to handle bullying situations among school-aged children effectively. Some schools are taking steps to improve this. I interviewed a middle school principal for this book and she shared with me an interesting way in which her school is now dealing with Bullies.

In this example, they used part shame and part peer pressure with a girl who was bullying her classmates. They assembled all the kids in one room and then the teacher and the school psychologist described in vivid detail the things the Bully had been doing. As they did this, they could see in the faces of the other students their distaste for what they were hearing. They could also see the discomfort of the Bully as she realized she had been found out and watched her power base disappear.

The good news is that the issue of bullying in schools is receiving so much attention and publicity these days and is recognized as the damaging behavior it is. The recent plethora of media attention won't make it go away but it will increase general awareness of the behavior.

SILVER LINING

Clearly this is a complex and personal subject. But there is a very bright spot for me in all of this. I am sure that had I not been bullied as a child I would not have achieved what I did in my life, both personally and professionally. It made me tougher and very determined that despite my differences, real or perceived, I would work harder to excel at whatever it was I set out to accomplish.

Someone recently mentioned to me that he continues to be surprised at how I am "always reinventing myself with no boundaries." Perhaps that reinvention muscle was developed as a response to the bullying.

THE BULLY

ADVICE SUMMARY

My best advice about how to manage the Type that is the Bully is to:

- Be aware that bullying shows up in your professional life and in the workplace.
- Stay close to your people and learn to recognize it is happening.
- Pause, when you feel bullied, to check the reality of the situation.
- Don't just retreat, because you cannot remedy things that way.
- Be in command of your reactions.
- Learn to distinguish between competitive people and Bullies.
- Act quickly to stop it.

CHAPTER 16

THE LONE RANGER - SELF-CONTAINED

COUNTRY HOUSE, CONNECTICUT. It's Sunday morning. I'm sitting on the porch of my house on the side of a mountain. I'm doing what I love: spending peaceful time alone and recharging from a busy week in New York City. My dogs are at my feet. My yoga instructor arrives in an hour. I'm feeling somewhat spiritual in this beautiful setting. This is what it means to pause, breathe and reflect. Life is good.

Because I often enjoy spending time alone in the evenings and on weekends, I sometimes think of myself as a recluse. My friends object to that idea, pointing out that I am unusually good at keeping in touch with people and staying up with the latest trends. They note that I always seem to be connecting one person with another. So I admit to being a trendy, sometimes outgoing introvert, with a very strong commitment to the development of others.

I understand this may seem like a contradiction. It is the case that being an introvert is very different from being a recluse, even though both tend to shy away from social interaction. Many introverts are very successful and well-respected managers and leaders.

SELF-CONTAINED

Please don't confuse an introvert with the Type that I call the Lone Ranger. I prefer to describe the Lone Ranger as someone who is "self-contained." Typically, he has limited connection with other people and is most comfortable working on his own.

We've all run into someone like this in school or in the neighborhood. He is the one who keeps to himself, rarely speaks up, has to be drawn out by the teacher or the coach or the club leader. She may have trouble making friends because she isn't comfortable extending herself. When he's in a social setting, on the playground or at a birthday party, he slips away on his own. Often, she'll say she'd rather read a book than go out with friends.

The Lone Ranger's self-contained and self-reliant behaviors can make her seem aloof and that may result in those around her feeling rebuffed. When this occurs in a team setting, it can lead to problems. If she disregards the need to support others or to contribute to the project, the others believe she isn't concerned with the success of the enterprise. This weakens the overall strength of the team.

CHARACTERISTICS

Recognizing a Lone Ranger can be relatively easy. The characteristics of this Type are that they tend to:

- Prefer to do things on their own.
- Avoid sharing.
- Be uncommunicative.
- Have difficulty with feedback.
- Claim a success as belonging to them alone or, if they don't have success, even claim the success of others as their own.

There are a few clues that can help you peg someone as a Lone Ranger in the interview process. If he is not forthcoming in his answers to your questions, you have a flag that there may be a communication problem. This should lead you to flush out his history with and his attitude toward teamwork. Pay attention to the personal pronouns he uses. Someone who always uses "I" is innately not team-focused. "I fixed the problem" and "I raised the revenue levels" are not the expressions of someone who is a team player. Listen for "we" and if you don't hear it, you have a good indication that you may be talking with a Lone Ranger.

Check with the other interviewers to see if they picked up similar signs. When I think I may have a Lone Ranger interviewing for a job, I like to check the references personally. Sometimes a simple comment, such as "He's always very focused on his work" or "She's very productive on her own" can lead to a revelation that the candidate has Lone Ranger tendencies.

NOT A TEAM PLAYER

Helping a Lone Ranger participate on a team can be a challenge to teachers, coaches and leaders of all kinds. The essence of being a good collaborator is to work with others collectively toward a shared objective. A Lone Ranger, as a quiet, self-contained individual, typically is not good at this.

MANAGEMENT CHALLENGE

Usually someone of this Type knows he's a Lone Ranger and in most cases he prefers to be that way. My advice for managing people like this is to encourage their development by following the basic good management practices. Give them a chance. Don't saddle them with a negative judgment before you work with them to open up to the group, to learn how to communicate and to learn the rewards of teamwork.

It can be effective to assign a colleague to work closely with the Lone Ranger as a way to help him learn how to be a team player. He actually may not realize that he needs to depend on the contributions of others and that others are depending on him. He may not have learned that when his co-workers do well, generally the whole group does well and that the success of others can make him look even more grand.

LIKE FATHER AND GRANDFATHER

Back in the late 1990's, when I went to London to head up a global business, part of my assignment was to make lots of changes to a process that hadn't been modernized to reflect advancements in the industry. It was no surprise that, as I did this, I bumped heads with several people resistant to change. One particular individual gave me the most grief.

He was one of these "old boys" who had been doing his job exactly the same way as his father and grandfather had done for many years before him. I am sure they all wore the same clothes and hung out at the same clubs. They felt there was no need to change anything.

"We should do the trades with my mate," he'd say, referring to a fellow he'd always preferred to give the business. He insisted on doing it his way even though that was out of date and no longer effective. Nor was it in keeping with the new, more efficient and lower cost market practices that the rest of the team and the world were implementing.

What was even worse was that he persisted in this without regard to how his approach would have a negative impact on the other people in the group. He just expected my team to do things his way even if it meant financial harm to the clients of those around him. He was devoted to the way things "had always been done" in the past, based on that old boys' ethic.

This one was easy for me to solve. I ignored his wishes and did what was best for all our clients, including his. He complained to my leader. Once the noise started, I was easily able to validate my reasons to all who questioned. A Lone Ranger who is just stuck in the past is easy to expose and easy to remove. You just need facts.

COMMUNICATE

Even if a Lone Ranger is producing stellar results or getting great grades, that alone does not exempt him from becoming a management challenge. In my opinion, if you are the parent, teacher, coach, manager or leader of any kind, the best thing you can do for the Lone Ranger is to encourage him to develop his communication skills. These can be learned. The more practice the better.

It is particularly important to establish a requirement for the Lone Ranger to give you regular updates on his work. You can use these meetings for frequent coaching. As you do this, give plenty of direct, honest, balanced feedback.

You may find it particularly difficult to get the Lone Ranger to accept your feedback. If that happens, you have an indicator of the severity of the challenge. Most importantly, you don't want to discourage the Lone Ranger from speaking, especially to you.

As a Lone Ranger pursues the development of his speaking abilities, he may also increase his confidence in interacting with others. With encouragement and practice, he can perhaps build a stronger understanding of the benefits of the team dynamic.

CAMOUFLAGE

As a result of his strong preference to be on his own, the Lone Ranger may go to some lengths to keep off the radar of his manager and others in his group. This may be unintentional and just an extension of his personality. Or it may be a deliberate strategy to avoid discomfort.

QUIET SUFFERER

There is one kind of Lone Ranger who takes cover in camouflage. She is quite the opposite of the Fluffer. She may be super smart and really capable but is held back because she is a weak communicator. By definition, such a person is a poor advocate for herself and may end up wasting her career hoping to be noticed and rewarded. In this Lone Ranger's eyes, a Fluffer can be an object of derision. She may even scorn the smooth talker as a bag of hot air. Most often, the truth is that she is jealous of the Fluffer's abilities to promote himself and his causes.

An employee like this can present a problem to her manager because her silence can serve to limit the success of the organization just as much as the hot air of the windbag does. The quiet employee makes it hard for the manager to see her abilities and therefore to make optimal use of them. The downside is that roles she might have performed brilliantly may be assigned to less capable people.

Sometimes, this individual may also seem to resemble an Underperformer but that may not be the case. The manager of this quiet employee has the tough challenge of seeing what is not easily visible. You must make an extra effort to draw her out in order to find out what's there. This is made easier when you follow the advice to stay close to your people by working in the fields.

If you find that she is high performing but lacks the flair to speak convincingly to others, you can arrange for her to have training to develop the skill. Even better, make it a job requirement so the group can benefit from what she has to offer. Remember that the best single thing you can do to help your child, student or employee find success is to help them strengthen and make use of their communication skills.

HIDING OUT

You may have an employee who acts like a Lone Ranger but is really trying to hide the fact that he is not doing his job well, hoping no one notices. This may be a calculated effort to mask his lack of ability. This is the Lone Ranger adopting the behaviors of the Underperformer, who knows he is bad at what he does. He may employ the Underperformer tactic of shunning the team to conceal the truth. He goes off on his own to shield his substandard work from the view of the others.

A manager who is paying attention will notice this. Other members of the group may alert him to the behavior as well. Lone Rangers of this sort should be managed in the same way you would manage an Underperformer. You need to make him speak, check for outside issues and figure out when you need to seek a different role for him.

MISTRUST

I had a Lone Ranger as a colleague when I was living in London. He was a nice enough fellow but had a quirky personality that gave you the sense that he was up to something underhanded. His self-interest always seemed to come before his contributions to the group and we never really felt we could trust him.

One fair summer's morning, he told his co-workers that he was going to a conference for the day. As it happened, another member of his team had taken that day off to go to the horse races at Ascot. What a surprise at the racecourse when he saw the very colleague who'd said he was going to a conference! Of course, this greatly reinforced the group's lack of trust.

If you can't trust someone, you really can't depend on him as part of your team. It is time to move him out.

SELF-PROMOTER

In his own opinion, what's good for the Lone Ranger comes before everything else. This Type tends to be focused solely on his own goals. It may be that such people can produce and even be top performers, but at what cost?

OUT FOR HIMSELF

When a Lone Ranger is also an Outperformer he can be very much dedicated to, and find great joy in, his own accomplishments. He can sometimes feel he is so good at what he does that he decides to head out on his own, ignoring everyone else. When this happens, the cohesiveness of the group weakens. This is the time to take the opportunity to teach the star the importance of teamwork.

If there is no improvement, such an individual should not be made part of a team and should never be moved into a position as leader or manager. The Lone Ranger needs to work alone. He might be moved to a role where he can function independently. If such a position does not exist within his current organization then the individual should be moved on.

The behavior of a Lone Ranger who pursues his own goals at the expense of others may at times be just like that of a Bully. Someone like this can actually turn out to be unmanageable. This requires decisive action by his leader.

SO SPECIAL

There are times when someone considers herself superior to the rest of the group, whether merited or not, and selects to behave as a Lone Ranger. This is similar to the Entitled individual, who may use the Lone Ranger stance as a way of pushing her sense of entitlement around, striking out on her own without regard for her co-workers. She does this as an intentional ploy to get the freedom to do as she likes, without consequence. This kind of Lone Ranger generally has a powerful ability for denial and will often reject criticism because she is so firm in her beliefs about her "specialness."

On the other hand, under her veneer of entitlement she may be insecure about her abilities. If this is so, she may also follow the route of the Lone Ranger as Underperformer who goes off on her own as a strategy to mask her shortcomings. Usually the cure for this is to move her out of the group.

THE LONE FLUFFER

The Fluffer version of the Lone Ranger Type likes to tell everyone how great she is and then do nothing to help the team accomplish the job. She is likely to portray herself as a hero, talk about her star quality and maneuver herself to be the center of attention.

Misrepresenting her abilities like this can make her a threat to the well being of the group. Believing that no one has figured out her game, she will charge ahead with her self-promotion program and become more and more confident until she makes a fatal mistake and is exposed.

People who are skilled at boasting can get ahead pretty quickly in the early days of a career. Eventually, however, they do have to produce convincingly. So in spite of their inflated sense of self, they are likely to get right-sized over time once they don't deliver. This may limit their future growth.

Another version of a Lone Ranger as Fluffer can be tough to manage for a different reason. These are people who say one thing and then do another. They are super personable and agreeable. They appear to be totally on board working in a collaborative environment. People want to like and trust them. Before long, reality sinks in.

I have worked with several such people over my many years but one seems to stay at top of mind. So many of us were initially very fond of this guy but we quickly and collectively noticed behaviors that made for trouble. We came to realize that all his agreeable camaraderie meant nothing. It was just his technique for complying with senior management's mandate that we work together.

We came to see a pattern where, after we left a meeting happy with the plan of action we had reached through compromise, our Lone Ranger friend just went ahead and did something else, whatever he wanted and in any way he desired. It was frustrating but I am sure not uncommon. The longer it went on, the worse things became. For the true collaborators in the business, it was demoralizing. Why bother?

This is the sort of Lone Ranger that motivated me to write a focused chapter on this Type. As the manager of a Lone Ranger like this, you have some control to correct the situation and you should take those steps right away. It is difficult when someone like this is your leader and also bad when one is a colleague. In both cases, you pretty much have to wait until senior management makes a move and that is typically not until after a bad situation becomes pretty obvious to all involved.

THE LONE RANGER AS LEADER

A strong leader recognizes the benefits of teamwork and relies on team dynamics to achieve great things. I am a big believer in letting those you manage be the ones who shine. The less I am in the spotlight and the more my charges are, the happier I am. I get tired of being around leaders who want to remind you of their greatness or those who want to make sure you know they are "better" than you. I have always believed that if you work hard and you willingly accomplish what is asked, you will move ahead.

The biggest challenge for a Lone Ranger to become an effective manager is to learn to acknowledge the contributions of his group regularly and sincerely. This will require considerable effort if he is not innately an inclusive team player. Usually such individuals will need to learn and work on ways to become more integrated with the group and perhaps more extroverted.

This doesn't mean they have to change who they are or abandon their own goals. Rather it is more a matter of changing some behaviors and ways of thinking. It means learning how to improve the way they speak to individuals and publicly to groups. It means making the effort to spend more time unifying with their team. It means intentionally putting themselves at the service of the group.

All of this can build trust, respect and camaraderie. In the right circumstances, when the Lone Ranger takes real pleasure in the accomplishments of his team, he can lead it to achieve great success. All ships rise together.

JOB SECURITY

I was and still am very fond of a guy I once managed who was a pretty good leader himself. He managed a business that required very specialized skills. He was excellent at making presentations to important clients and to senior management. He was a true subject matter expert and an asset to the firm.

The challenge for me as his leader was that he kept all the high profile activities exclusively for himself. It is never prudent to run a big global business with only one person capable of properly doing any given job. My colleague had built his group by surrounding himself with very competent technical experts, all of whom expressed little or no interest in running the client meetings or the internal presentations. Their leader was happy to keep it that way.

Every year I would challenge him to either train or hire someone who could at least be a reliable backup. Every year he would say, "I know." Yet nothing changed.

Time after time I'd say, "What if you get hit by a bus?" He'd reply, "Oh yes, you're right." Then he would do nothing about it.

By then, it was easy to see that this manager wanted to be the single public face of this business and its undisputed authority. It wasn't easy for me to "get tough" on this issue because I truly enjoyed working with this guy and his team seemed to like him as well. Eventually, we did ease another individual into taking on small portions of the external work but by the time I left this still had not been fully resolved.

This is an example of a kind of Lone Ranger who is focused on his own job protection. Job security isn't something I frequently thought about in connection with highly paid leaders working in technical businesses. But everyone is human and can be insecure to some degree. Over my many years in the financial industry, I was often naively surprised at the number of people who spent significant amounts of time orchestrating their political position. There I was focusing on, and agreeing to do, things that I thought important for the success of the firm. I was typically also having fun. To this day, I am not sure who was smarter or more successful.

WILLING TO DELEGATE

The qualities of a Lone Ranger can sometimes work to his advantage as a manager. When a Lone Ranger has a self-starter in his group, he may be more willing than other managers to let her pursue her ideas on her own. Being willing to delegate to team members can be a strong plus and can make the people who work for such a leader feel that they truly own their success. These employees are typically happy and loyal.

As he delegates, it is essential that the Lone Ranger understand that he owns the leadership role and that he does not try to subcontract his responsibilities for the team to someone else.

Unfortunately, some Lone Ranger leaders may feel threatened by employees who take initiative or ask for increased responsibilities. Such leaders are high achievers who fail to derive pleasure from the great accomplishments of those they manage. They are unwilling to delegate and may feel the need to keep others at bay in order to protect their own job. They are terrible at succession planning. If a Lone Ranger has these tendencies, she may not ever be a suitable leader.

The best leaders are those who genuinely find great happiness in the success of those around them and the overall organization. They recognize that teamwork and collective achievement are the route to success and the best way for them to reach their own goals. When this happens, it's a success story all around.

THE LONE RANGER
ADVICE SUMMARY

My best advice about how to manage the Type that is the Lone Ranger is to:

- Make them speak.
- Help them embrace the need for teamwork.
- Require them to develop communication skills.
- Figure out if they're hiding poor performance.
- Recognize when you need to move them out.

A PLACE FOR EVERYONE

C H A P T E R   1 7

THE DIFFERENCES

SINGAPORE. I am sitting in a conference room with about six people I have just met in person for the first time. Their primary job is to sell the financial products developed by my various teams throughout the world. We are discussing progress and business results and the local group is giving me feedback and suggestions for improvements.

One of the participants is a super bright and successful young Asian woman who wants to discuss one of my employees in her region. She is four feet, nine inches tall and looks to me like an 18-year-old girl. In front of the entire assembled group, she barks at me, "For years I am being told the issue with Priscilla is a language problem but let me tell you, it is much more than just a language problem!"

Her direct frankness startles my male American ears. In the U.S. and the U.K, this kind of harsh personal criticism would be made more privately. Here it is being given

217

in a roomful of people. Equally surprising is the source. This is not the sort of thing you would typically expect to be hearing from someone who looks like a young girl, nor, in my experience, from an Asian person of any age. However, the facts are that she holds a senior, client facing position and is a mother of two. I hadn't expected her to be this aggressive. It is yet another lesson for me about how things are so often not what you expect and a great example of how you need to be conscious all the time of differences among people.

When you manage a diverse global population of high achievers, you learn quickly that you need to be flexible and resourceful in your approach. There is not just one convention or procedure or standard operating model that works well in all cultures and circumstances.

It may be easier to recognize this in a global context, yet if you think about it, even on a local level being alert to differences is important for parents managing their children, a teacher managing a class or a general managing his troops. My sister is an elementary school teacher in a city school in Philadelphia where every third kid is from a different country. She has to be sensitive to diversity issues every day.

THERE IS NO NORMAL

I am not normal. I have never claimed to be and believe me, many people have reminded me of this throughout my life. There are so many times I have been accused of being crazy, whifty or strange that I could write another book just on that topic.

My sanity was questioned back when I decided to move to New York City because no one we ever knew back in Philadelphia had done that. Then when I got to New York, my colleagues found it strange that I thought

New Jersey was a great place to live. Where I grew up in Philadelphia, moving to New Jersey meant you had "made it" and could afford a "single home," as opposed to a "row house" where we lived.

Speaking of the Garden State, try traveling to Europe with someone who thinks "normal" is defined by how things are done in New Jersey. I was once in a lovely sandwich shop in Geneva, Switzerland, getting lunch with one such character. The shop sold mozzarella cheese packaged in a box shaped like a cottage. Upon seeing what I thought was quaint and clever packaging, my friend blurted out, "That's not normal!" I was stunned. The sweet, old Italian merchant was speechless. Perhaps he didn't understand English. Let us hope.

Another example I love is that of a young Black woman who had grown up in Atlanta. I knew she was the right person for our group right after the company hired her. In her orientation she was asked the question, "Who is the person you would most like to be?" Her answer was, "Beyonce." She was completely sincere in admiring this talented Black superstar who had created an entire brand around herself and achieved huge success. This young woman didn't invoke the traditional, more staid examples. She was able to go beyond the surface of her new daily life to what she saw as the essence of success.

What is the moral of this story? Don't make assumptions. It's another argument in favor of the need to be open to differences, value variety and to find ways to reap the associated benefits.

THE NEW ELEPHANT

Being sensitive to differences is important as we manage people, teach students and interact with one another. I have learned so much from my experiences around the world as a manager – with my superiors and with colleagues, as well as with the many people I have met through my yoga practice. I have had failures and successes in all kinds of situations. I have learned about how people behave differently in similar circumstances and how others can view widely varying situations the same way.

Never underestimate what may be considered "different" or "acceptable." At one point over the last several years, I gained some weight. In the U. S., people might not be too quick to highlight that for you. In Hong Kong, a woman colleague came right up to me and said, "I was looking at you from the side. You need to exercise more."

In London, when I went to visit someone senior in the firm, his greeting was to look me up and down and say, "You look prosperous." I inquired if he meant I had gained weight. I was right. Here in America, we would most likely wait to say these things until after the new elephant had left the room!

PROGRESS?

In the mid-1990s, I was appointed the first head of the Diversity Committee of my division of my firm. In those days, much of the corporate world was making efforts to address diversity issues and make the workplace more inclusive for valuable talent. I have always thought I was selected for this role because of my ability to fit into unfamiliar situations. This was not long after I got my reputation for being "The Fixer." I had just come back from spending two years in London restructuring a global business.

WORK FROM HOME?

Our Committee's focus was mainly on women's concerns and a little bit about African-American issues. One of our first actions was to set up a pilot project that would become a framework for allowing selected people to work from home. This was also in the very early days of remote technology, so it did require some effort and coordination with many groups of people.

We chose a group of about 15 employees to participate. We consciously did not pick only women with young children because we did want to be "inclusive" and we didn't want the males in charge to discount our efforts as some baby-sitting replacement strategy. One guy we chose had a role that was research driven: making calls to companies, doing analysis and generating recommendations. Also, his wife had recently given birth to twins. He went to his boss to explain what we had proposed and asked her which day of the week she thought might be best for him to work from home. Her response was, "Sunday."

NOT SO MUCH

It's about 20 years since I ran that first Diversity Committee. I am not real sure we have come that far in our thinking. Things are better, but by how much?

I can give you a recent personal experience that tells me how, although we may have made some progress, many corporate types still remain uncomfortable talking about this subject. It happened when I gave an early draft of this book to a group of business people to read. It turned out that most of the issues and objections they raised were with this section about the differences among people, which at the time contained a more extensive discussion of this topic.

My own view is that people in business organizations have become paranoid that their progress is not as great as they would like you to believe. As a consequence, they consider it better policy to just avoid the conversation.

I believe when we ask for data demonstrating progress in this area, in most parts of the world the metrics may not stand up to the anecdotes.

STRAIGHT, MARRIED, WHITE GUYS

Face it. When you pause and take a good look around, you see that the world is overwhelmingly run by straight, married, white guys. Especially in business but also in lots of other fields a great majority of the top people fit into this category. This may not be true about large domestic organizations in places like Japan, China, India or Brazil but they do tend to be solely populated mainly by people of local ethnicity.

My perspective is from my experience working at a large, multinational corporation headquartered in the U.S. My familiarity extends to my firm's global competitors based in North America, Europe and Asia and, to a somewhat lesser degree, in Latin America, the Middle East and Australia. I have spent many years traveling to far parts of the globe and working in the fields with all kinds of people at all levels. My observations come from that experience and while they are not based on any kind of rigorous research, certain things seem obvious to me and worthy of mention.

From my vantage point, everyone other than straight, married, white guys is "different" by definition. This includes women, gays, single people, older people, Asians, Indians, Blacks and others who are minorities in their environments. There has recently been lots of attention given to hurdles that introverts have to get over in order to be recognized and promoted. Certainly we could all come up with other particular groups.

BEYOND TOLERANCE

Nowadays, being sensitive to many kinds of diversity is recognized as important. There are programs designed to enhance tolerance but I say that concept falls short of the mark. I think we need to go beyond being "tolerant" to increasing the acceptance of, and even seeking out, those who are "different."

There is a lot of work still to do to ensure open opportunity for everyone. There are many complexities to our differences. Each group has unique issues based on history, education and cultural norms.

I believe that what worked for me to overcome biases can be helpful to any group in overcoming discrimination and gaining opportunities. What worked for me was simply that strong work ethic. The most valuable guidance a parent, teacher, employer or leader of any kind can give is to encourage your employees or students or children to be willing to work hard to get the job done, no matter what it takes. If you have basic ability, that willingness to work hard can make all the difference. As I say, I'll take attitude over ability every time.

But that is still only part of the solution. As managers and leaders who run organizations of all kinds, we need to make sure that we are closely in touch with those we lead and that we communicate all opportunities effectively. This calls for us to develop the skills to gain insight into diverse ethnic groups and cultures. We have the responsibility to be sensitive to the full range of differences among all kinds of people, encourage their teamwork, give honest and timely feedback and manage their expectations realistically.

Doing this well requires flexibility and resourcefulness and it's among the most challenging aspects of being a leader. It is also one of the most interesting.

CHAPTER 18

A PLACE FOR EVERYONE

NEW YORK CITY, NEW YORK. I am in Central Park. It is very early in the morning and I am walking my two Labs, Stella and Azeet, as I do every day before going to work. I have been a member of the dog-walking brigade for many years. It's slow going these days because this is quite an elderly pair.

The very first pet I ever had in my life was a wonderfully gentle yellow Labrador retriever named Martha. She was so much a peaceful soul that often people would come up to her on the street and ask if they could just hug her. Martha passed away on May 4, 2008. I was left with a seven-year-old black Lab named Stella who became depressed as she was missing her soul mate. I quickly set about looking for a new companion for Stella and myself by contacting various Labrador retriever rescue organizations.

My goal was to find a young black female Labrador to be Stella's partner. I went the rescue route because Labs are popular dogs with families with children and, unfortunately, many such families don't always appreciate the work that is needed to train those cute little puppies. As a result, many wonderful Labs end up with the rescue groups. I wanted young so that I could establish a sort of age cycle with my dogs, as I thought I would always have two. I wanted black because I thought it would be nice to be able to finally choose furniture, sheets and car interior of a color that would not show dog hair. When you have a both a black and a yellow Lab, one or the other's hair shows up no matter what you choose!

So I went in search of a young black female Lab. What I got was an old yellow male!

A worker at one of the rescue organizations asked if I would be a foster parent for a week for a nine-year-old yellow male. I was to return the dog to her rescue facility at the weekend. The yellow fellow arrived at my building in New York City on a Monday. He was accompanied by his 17-year-old brother (human) and the boy's father. The family was moving to Israel and they were unable to take their pet with them. They had been trying to find a home for him for several months. After having no success with all their searching and calling, they had reluctantly contacted a rescue organization, hoping they could find a suitable home. It didn't take me more than about five minutes to know how this search would resolve itself.

That old guy is now very old and is the happiest living thing I have ever encountered in my life. He immediately bonded with Stella and even with my cat and yes, he took my heart and wrapped himself around it. As I write this, he is lying by my feet. He is now 14 years old, completely deaf and riddled with all sorts of senior ailments but he is still happy and grateful to make us all happy too.

I am so glad his original family cared so much about getting him to a really good home. I remain in contact with them and send them pictures often. This family knew that there had to be a place suitable for what this old boy had to offer and they worked really hard to find it.

FIND THE RIGHT PLACE

I've offered up a recipe to identify and foster good employees, students and children help them move on to succeed. I've described certain Types of people and how to be most effective in working with each of them and the opportunities in promoting diversity.

My final advice is perhaps the single most important point for parents, teachers, coaches, managers and leaders of all kinds. It is to encourage you to learn to identify the talents that each individual possesses and then work to match those strengths and interests to a sport, hobby, class or role that will best leverage them.

Even as I earned my reputation as "The Ax Man," I always made it a priority to help usher departing members of a group to a place where they could go on to do well. I felt that was my responsibility as a good manager. Many of those individuals are still in regular contact with me today. When you get it right, great performance, satisfaction and happiness will follow. I speak from experience. It works.

To do this with strong performers who are motivated and eager to learn can be straightforward and rewarding. Still, some people find it hard to let their stars go. They prefer to keep great talent near at hand. I consider this a disservice to the individual and the organization. The ability to launch a star is always the sign of a great leader.

It's when you have problem performers that the challenge grows. If you really want to be an effective parent, teacher or manager, you can't just take your problem people and cast them away, although too many do try to pass off their problems to others. The challenge is to assess carefully, think hard and become creative to help get those individuals to a better place.

As a responsible parent, you have little choice but to do this as best you can. As a manager, it is one of the best things you can do for a struggling employee. If you have little or no interest in making that kind of effort, perhaps you need to do some assessing and creative thinking for yourself and find a better match for your own interests. Perhaps managing others is not for you?

WORKING YOUR WAY THROUGH

A mismatch of a person's talent to a task or their abilities to a job's requirements is destructive for that person, their family and their class, their team or their organization. Usually what happens is that great skills are wasted and important jobs are not performed well.

The good leader's responsibility is to move the child, student or employee from the mismatched role and into one that is more suitable. This almost inevitably means finding your way through some tough moments. It's not always easy to admit that something is wrong. Denial can kick in and it can be a delicate matter to find the way to communicate effectively with the person involved.

The most helpful way to work through this kind of circumstance, as I've discovered through many difficult situations in my own work life, calls for three things.

1. Be direct and frequent with feedback, as I always recommend.

2. Be encouraging that there is a role that needs the benefit of the strengths of the person.

3. Work together with the individual to focus on those strengths and help him or her move to the chosen role.

I have always felt this to be a priority as a manager. I have done this many, many times. Here are three of my favorite examples.

WHEN BAU CHANGED

I once spent about 18 months working with a mid-career person I had inherited. She was in a role that was good for her when the requirements were about carrying out business as usual, which we called BAU. That was an environment where we took care of existing customers, sold them quality products and client demands were of the generally pleasant and often administrative sort. She was fully competent at the "administrivia" part of her role.

At some point while I was managing this individual the world shifted and we found ourselves with a suddenly inferior product. This meant we had significant challenges in keeping our clients informed and we faced the need to provide in-depth explanations about the turn in our fortunes. In other words, BAU changed dramatically. Unfortunately, this new environment was not one in which my charge could thrive. I was presented with many requests to make a change.

I believe to my credit, I spent lots of time discussing her recent performance with her. Part of me believed that the team wanted a scapegoat to blame for the degradation of the product's quality and that my subject was being set up to take the fall. I was valiantly trying to bring her up to speed. After many months of working closely with her, hoping to realize a change in her status, I concluded it was time to start providing this woman of specific talents with options to utilize her skills outside of her current group.

The process to accomplish this wasn't altogether smooth. My employee did not always embrace the feedback. Some of her critics changed their tune from time to time, making things more complex. None of this is unusual. The manager's job through such a transition is to remain clear, direct and closely involved. It is important to be encouraging and keep communication flowing.

The good news is that this colleague did eventually find her niche. She came to understand her strengths and the things she should steer clear of. She took a new position well matched to her abilities and to this day, more than ten years later, she remains successful and continues to thrive.

THE RIGHT FIT, WITH NO BELT

Another time, I managed a rather homogeneous group of white males. We had one young black man and one young woman on the team but all of the senior people were white men. The client base had a largely similar make up, so my employees and their clients were most likely all feeling pretty comfortable with each other as they went about their business. (I realize this situation was loaded with all sorts of opportunities to shift away from this sameness and be assured in some ways I did make progress.)

Enter a new member of the team. He was somewhat different from the existing members of our boys' club. Some of this guy's "difference" came from his ethnicity. He also had a particular style to his appearance that was very clearly not the fashion of the rest of the team. There were other differences - in work habits, writing style and other behaviors - that were not sitting well with the other kids on the playground. Many of the group noted things like the fact that he rarely wore a belt and had a sales manner that was less "formal finance" and more "used car salesman."

Early on, it became clear to me that I was going to need to do something extra to help our new guy integrate into the team. It wasn't going to happen naturally. Some of the team members made an effort to help; others did not. Those others stayed snug in their shared cozy alignment as pretty similar white guys with similar outside lifestyles and similar ways of relating with the clients.

Next, enter a new business for the team to serve. Miracles do happen! The new business involved selling to clients who were less old boys' club and more pedestrian in their ways. In fact, these new clients were somewhat suspect of the "old boys," who could occasionally be thought to talk down to this powerful and profitable new customer base.

I knew my "different" guy was exactly the right fit for this new order. He had the right conversational style and other strengths that were well suited for working with this client population. He related well to these customers and knew how to make them feel like they were the most important people in the world. I joked with my outlier colleague that perhaps I did want him to dress more like a car salesman than a fancy banker. We laughed together about getting him a plaid sports coat to wear to his client meetings. We may even have done it.

Fast forward to today. This same "outsider" is now a major voice in his industry and is prominent in the media, where people follow his recommendations closely. I like to think that I played some part in getting him started in his niche, which he then went on to develop brilliantly. When I hear him on the radio, I always think of the plaid jacket and imagine him speaking to an adoring crowd in a large conference room off some highway in New Jersey. I don't know if he now wears a belt with any regularity.

ON YOUR OWN

One of the most talented people who ever worked for me was actually a member of the same team that Mr. Plaid Jacket joined. I knew from the start that he was a star and when I left that group to move on to a completely different part of the organization, I was quickly able to get him a spot in my new business. This wasn't difficult, because others easily recognized his talents too. I always found him a major asset.

A couple of years later, I gave up my position to take some time off. He stayed and, in my opinion, hit a rocky road that wasn't merited. There came a time when he and another colleague were both promised an increase in compensation. The other guy got it; he did not. This was when he showed us all how a good attitude and resourcefulness can help an individual find his own place, even through circumstances that seem unfair. He began a search, left the company for a competing firm and immediately got his momentum. He has now been promoted to a senior management position there and is thriving.

Through it all - rejection, move, merit promotion, becoming a proud father and even a battle with serious illness - he's kept his good humor and the most positive outlook you'll ever see. I always look forward to being in touch with him and I see him as a great example of how to take responsibility into your own hands. He just goes with things as they happen and finds his way to make the best out of them. By depending on his positive, go-ahead attitude, he found his own place that is right for him.

TRY AND TRY AGAIN

There are many ways people figure out how to find the right place all on their own, outside of the framework of an organization or class and without the benefit of guidance from a manager or teacher. My own sister is another great example of what it can take to pull that off.

When she found herself divorced and a single mother raising her son, she went to college at night. She got a job in Health Care Administration and, after several years, found out that she didn't like it at all. She performed the job well but she became pretty unhappy with it and couldn't see herself there for the long term. She understood clearly that this was not the right place for her.

So she made the decision to go back to school another time to get a graduate degree, again at night while working during the day. This time she chose the completely different field of education. She stuck with it, earned her degree and became a happy elementary school teacher. Now she is remarried, her first son is an adult with a family of his own and her young son has grown to become a very promising fellow in high school. She loves her work. She found her right place and did it all on her own.

MESSY REAL WORLD

How to help someone find the right place may not always be obvious. Sometimes, the right way to move a person on to success is to move him out of a role he is trying to perform well but for which he is not well suited. It can be especially difficult when you are dealing with the challenges of a problem employee but I firmly believe it is always worth it to try.

As you work your way through the difficulties, you learn to trust that there really is a future outcome that is better than the current problem situation. When he becomes accomplished in his new place, he will grow to appreciate your help.

TYPES CAN HELP

Having insight into what Type someone is can be a big help in guiding him to a place he can find rewarding. Sometimes, in the messy real world, you will find yourself managing people who are not cleanly one Type or another, but a combination of Types. When you are faced with this, your challenge is compounded. But still, there is a place for everyone.

For example, consider an Outperformer who is Entitled. You know you don't have to worry about his performance; you do need to help cure him of his sense of entitlement. Once he is free of that, his talents and skills can take precedence in his finding the right place.

Consider a Fluffer who is a Bully. Because her bullying overshadows her performance, she may appear to be an Underperformer. Helping her to see and change her bullying ways and challenging her to come through with more than talk and intimidation, may uncover her strong capabilities. When that has happened, maybe she will need a clean start with a group who hasn't experienced her as a Bully.

Consider an Underperformer who is also an Unmanageable. It could be that this one causes trouble and discord as a way to cover up his poor performance. This is when to look for a mismatch. Perhaps the work he has been assigned in your group is not the right fit for him and you can help him find another position.

OTHER MANAGERS CAN HELP

Experience with the various Types will prove a big aid in finding the right place for each individual. If you haven't had direct experience with a particular Type yourself, I recommend turning to your colleagues for suggestions and support. I have needed such help with all the Types characterized in this book. You can reciprocate and do the same for other managers in turn.

There are plenty of ways you may do well to get help from others in finding a good place for your charge. I told the story of a problem team member who became unmanageable and disrupted my world badly and I was immensely grateful for help from another manager. It took that help to find a positive solution where the individual could be productive. I refer to that experience because I believe that finding the right match of person and role can solve even an extreme situation like that one. We all just need to breathe, be patient and get help from others.

A PLACE FOR EVERYONE

Yes, I do believe that there is a right place for everyone. There was for me.

There was a time when I used to say that I was "the son of a Postman from the ghetto of Philadelphia." Understandably, this annoyed my parents and they were right to be annoyed. Years ago, I arrived at the recognition of just how valuable my early years were and the strength of the foundation that they built for me. My long career at a prominent global company seemed unlikely when I was growing up in that old neighborhood. When I took my first position as a junior analyst, who could have predicted the remarkable journey I was starting or where I would end up? Who knows what path any child will travel with the right support and guidance?

Helping someone find his or her way is, for me, the best part of any job. I consider it a badge of a good manager, teacher, parent or any other kind of leader to make a practice of finding a place for each person where he or she can contribute and thrive.

I am applying these principles to my own life now as I make my way to a new place. I know it will include spending time on writing, animal welfare, teaching and sharing my life with those who are less fortunate than I have been.

The Labs are now in their places back home, resting from their walk in the park. I am on my way to the office for an early morning meeting. I once noted that I am over-scheduled, over-challenged and over-fortunate. I could not ask for more. To be over-scheduled is a small price for being able to work in the fields and establish rich long-term relationships with people. Being over-challenged is the benefit of encountering diversity up close and learning how to handle "two Caesars." I started out resolved to "do whatever it takes" and I feel more than fortunate that I have managed to deliver, as the son of a Postman.

AFTERWORD

Since I left the corporate world, I have launched several new endeavors. True to my "rule of threes," I am pursuing three primary interests.

1. I am writing, speaking and teaching about leadership, management and personal development. This involves formal presentations to assorted kinds of groups as well as continued mentoring of individuals in all parts of the world. I'm continuing my blog, sonofapostman. com, and am already working on my next book.

2. I am sharing my life's lessons with high school students and young adults, offering guidance as they make decisions about their futures. Still closely in touch with my own rise from a working-class youth, I meet with inner-city kids in school settings and after-school programs, helping them think about job and career choices and coaching them to develop strong interviewing skills.

3. As a yogi, I practice meditation and am an increasingly serious student of mindfulness. In the past, I've tended to live my life in at least third gear. Now I am becoming better at finding ways to downshift, at least sometimes, allowing space for a more focused awareness of my life. Increasingly, I am incorporating mindfulness into my other interests as well.

It is typical that I have ambitions that involve varied roles. In my former career, I was often simultaneously responsible for several businesses that were completely unrelated. I am still a skillful plate spinner! Finding the interconnections among roles and among people has been and continues to be a source of satisfaction for me and I find that others appreciate it.

One of my new goals is to avoid giving people more pressure than they already feel. I think this is a worthy objective and one that I regularly preach to myself as well. I am proud that I can now distinguish better what things matter the most and recognize that many other things are not necessary at all. I am finding that this makes room for new possibilities.

ACKNOWLEDGMENT

Thanks to Nancy P Macagno, who was a close friend long before I decided to write this book. She also happens to be a talented and experienced editor. I considered it a truly special thing that a friend became my editor because it's so important to me that my "voice" be reflected in my writing. Nancy totally understood how to make that happen because she has listened to my voice for many years!

We also had a ton of fun and who doesn't want to have fun when you are working and spending so much time together!

ABOUT THE AUTHOR

Kevin R Alger, CFA, enjoyed a 32-year career at a prominent global financial services company where he held key leadership positions managing numerous businesses and thousands of people worldwide. He became well known as the go-to guy for advice and practical, no-non-sense guidance about leadership and managing people and remains a favorite mentor and role model.

In 2013 he left his position as a senior executive to join the growing movement for social good. A seasoned yoga practitioner and a seeker of mindfulness, Kevin is creative in applying his knowledge and beliefs to support young people as they launch into their working lives and adulthood. As a speaker, he is a source of lively, helpful insights for business executives, teachers, parents, managers, coaches and leaders of all kinds and he regularly calls on his vast worldwide network to generate mutually positive introductions.

Kevin is a resident of New York City and rural Connecticut, where he is a long-time supporter of animal welfare organizations. He shares his latest observations in his blog at sonofapostman.com.

29496427R00155

Made in the USA
Charleston, SC
13 May 2014